Contents

How to use this book

This book provides three sets of exam papers that mirror the AQA GCSE exam papers.

The audio, teacher-examiner parts (for Paper 2: Speaking), model answers and mark schemes can be accessed using the QR codes throughout the book or by visiting www.oxfordsecondary.co.uk/aqagcse-french-pp.

The exam papers contain hints and tips. The first set of papers provides tips for all questions and all skills, in order to help you gain confidence in answering questions. In the second set of papers there are fewer tips for listening and reading. The third set of papers does not contain tips, so that you have an opportunity to practise answering questions independently in an exam situation.

AQA GCSE French Higher

AQA GCSE French is made up of four exam papers, each with a weighting of 25% towards the final mark. The Foundation Tier is for students targeting Grades 1-5 and the Higher Tier is for students targeting Grades 4-9. For more details about the specification and for the most up-to-date assessment information, please see the AQA website.

Paper 1: Listening

There are 45 minutes to complete the Higher listening paper and 50 marks available. In Section A, the questions are in English and the answers required will either be non-verbal or in English. In Section B, the questions are in French and the answers required will either be non-verbal or in French.

The time includes 5 minutes at the start of the exam to read through the paper. Practise reading through the paper in this time. You may need to skim-read to get all the way through it, but try to use the time in a focused way. Identify the questions where you need to give several answers about the audio passage, or more than one piece of information, so that you're ready to listen out for the details you need. It's also good to read Section B carefully to make sure you understand the questions being asked.

The level of difficulty varies throughout the paper so don't lose heart if you encounter a hard question early on, as it doesn't mean you will find the questions that follow even harder. In AQA GCSE Paper 1, there are some questions that appear both on the Foundation and Higher Tier papers.

Use the tips in the Set 1 and Set 2 listening papers in this book to build your confidence in exam technique and to help you listen out for the correct answers.

Paper 2: Speaking

There are 60 marks available for the speaking paper. For Higher Tier, you will have supervised preparation time of 12 minutes followed by an exam of 10-12 minutes.

There are three parts to the exam:

- Role-play (15 marks) – this will last approximately 3 minutes for Higher Tier

- Photo card (15 marks) – this will last approximately 2 minutes for Higher Tier

- General Conversation (30 marks) – this will last between 5-7 minutes for Higher Tier

The candidate chooses one theme for the general conversation and the other theme will be the one that hasn't been covered in the photo card. Here is a chart showing the possible test sequences based on the candidate's choice of theme:

Role-play	Candidate's chosen conversation theme	Photo card	Candidate's second conversation theme
1, 2 or 3	Theme 1: Identity and culture	B	Theme 3
		C	Theme 2
	Theme 2: Local, national, international and global areas of interest	A	Theme 3
		C	Theme 1
	Theme 3: Current and future study and employment	A	Theme 2
		B	Theme 1

Each paper in this book contains a role-play and a photo card from each theme. The teacher-examiner part and two marked sample responses for each can be found online. For general conversation, there are two marked sample responses included in the book for each paper, followed by tasks to complete, with the following combinations of themes:

- Set 1 covers Themes 1 and 2

- Set 2 covers Themes 2 and 3

- Set 3 covers Themes 3 and 1

Tips are provided for the role-plays and photo cards in the Set 1 and Set 2 speaking papers in this book. These will help you respond more fully to the questions asked and anticipate the unexpected questions.

Paper 3: Reading

There is 1 hour to complete the Higher reading paper, with 60 marks available. In Section A, the questions are in English and the answers required will either be non-verbal or in English. In Section B, the questions are in French and the answers required will either be non-verbal or in French. Different types of written texts are used in the reading paper, including literary extracts. In this book, example answers are given if further guidance is needed on how to answer a question, so watch out for these.

The level of difficulty varies throughout the paper so don't lose heart if you encounter a hard question early on as it doesn't mean you will find the questions that follow even harder. In AQA GCSE Paper 3, there are some questions that appear both on the Foundation and Higher Tier papers.

In Section C, there is a translation from French into English of a minimum of 50 words.

Use the tips in the Set 1 and Set 2 reading papers in this book to build your confidence in exam technique and to help you pick out the correct answers from the text.

Paper 4: Writing

There is 1 hour 15 minutes to complete the writing paper and 60 marks available. All answers should be written in French.

For Higher Tier there are three questions:

- Question 1 (16 marks): One of a choice of two structured writing tasks of 90 words, with a series of bullet points to cover in your response. In AQA GCSE Paper 4, this question is the same as question 4 on the Foundation Tier paper.

- Question 2 (32 marks): One of a choice of two writing tasks of 150 words, with a series of bullet points to cover in your response.

- Question 3 (12 marks): A translation from English into French/French/Spanish of a minimum of 50 words.

Tips are provided in the Set 1 and Set 2 writing papers in this book, to help you respond to the questions and to give guidance on extending your answers. Two marked model answers are included online for questions 1 and 2. Also included online is a mark scheme for question 3.

AQA GCSE French (9-1)

Higher Tier Paper 1 Listening

Time allowed: 45 minutes
(including 5 minutes' reading time before the test)

You will need no other materials.
The pauses are pre-recorded for this test.

Information
- The marks for the questions are shown in brackets. The maximum mark for this paper is 50.
- You must **not** use a dictionary.

Advice
This is what you should do for each item.
- After the question number is announced, there will be a pause to allow you to read the instructions and questions.
- Listen carefully to the recording and read the questions again.
- Listen to the recording again, and then answer the questions.
- When the next question is about to start you will hear a bleep.
- You may write at any time during the test.
- In **Section A**, answer the questions in **English**. In **Section B**, answer the questions in **French**.
- You must answer all the questions in the spaces provided. Do not write on blank pages.
- Write neatly and put down all the information you are asked to give.
- **You must not ask questions or interrupt during the test.**
- You have five minutes to read through the question paper. You may make notes during this time. You may turn to the questions now.
- **The test starts now.**

Listen to the audio

Please note: The Practice Paper questions and answers have not been written or approved by AQA.

Section A   Questions and answers in **English**

The weather forecast

You listen to the weather forecast on French radio.

Answer both questions.

> - Read the statements to prepare before you listen. The statements in question 01 concern the south of France and in question 02 the north of France, so you are likely to hear these geographical areas mentioned.
> - Expect some statements to be nearly true but not quite, e.g. will it be windy at the same time as it will be stormy? Or will it be windy before/ after the storm? Focus on subtle differences the second time you hear the recording.

0 1   Choose **one** statement that is **true**. Write the correct letter in the box.

A	There will be thunderstorms during the day in the south of France.
B	At the same time as the thunderstorms, it will be very windy.
C	People are advised to stay indoors.

[1 mark]

0 2   Choose **one** statement that is **true**. Write the correct letter in the box.

A	In the northern half of France, the weather has been calm recently.
B	There is a risk of a few showers.
C	The afternoon will be mainly cloudy.

[1 mark]

An environmental problem

You hear an interview on French radio about plastic pollution.

For each part of the interview, choose the correct description of what is discussed. Write the correct letter in the box.

> After reading the questions carefully, think about what vocabulary might be used for each option e.g. 03 *technologie/ urgence.*

0 3		
	A	An environmental issue that needs urgent solutions
	B	Some of the technological solutions to the problem

[1 mark]

0 4		
	A	How supermarkets can contribute to the war against plastics
	B	How fruit and vegetables are affected by the use of plastic

[1 mark]

0 5		
	A	The effect of plastic on aquatic species
	B	The recycling of certain types of plastics

[1 mark]

0 6		
	A	How private transport makes the problem worse
	B	What individuals and the government can do to address the issue

[1 mark]

An argument at home

You are staying at your exchange partner's home. You witness an argument between Luc and his mother.

Complete the sentences in **English**.

Answer both parts of question 7 and question 8.

> Read the question carefully for context. A teenager is having an argument with his mother. What could it be about?

| 0 7 . 1 | Luc is asking permission to _____.

[1 mark]

| 0 7 . 2 | He finds his mother's reaction unfair because

_____.

[1 mark]

| 0 8 . 1 | Luc's mother is concerned for _____.

[1 mark]

| 0 8 . 2 | What frustrates Luc is that his friend Thomas

_____.

[1 mark]

Survey on homework

Kévin is doing a survey on homework. What is the attitude of the four respondents towards homework?

For a negative opinion, write **N**.

For a positive opinion, write **P**.

For a positive and negative opinion, write **P+N**.

> Listen out for words that often introduce the opposite point of view, indicating an attitude that is both positive and negative, e.g. *mais*, *par contre*.

| 0 9 | Amélie | | **[1 mark]**

| 1 0 | Charles | | **[1 mark]**

| 1 1 | Lionel | | **[1 mark]**

| 1 2 | Delphine | | **[1 mark]**

The importance of marriage

While in France, you hear teenagers discussing the importance of marriage.

Answer the questions in **English**.

For all four questions, you can anticipate what is going to be said. However, make sure you listen carefully to the speakers. They may confirm what you thought or lead you to an unexpected answer.

| 1 | 3 | What uncertainty is the speaker referring to?

_____

[1 mark]

| 1 | 4 | In what circumstances does this speaker say getting married is essential?

_____

[1 mark]

| 1 | 5 | For this speaker, what is the main advantage of living together without getting married?

_____

[1 mark]

| 1 | 6 | What sort of commitment is marriage for this speaker?

_____

[1 mark]

Veganism

Listen to a French radio programme on veganism.

What is each person's attitude towards veganism?

For a negative opinion, write **N**.

For a positive opinion, write **P**.

For a positive and negative opinion, write **P+N**.

> Think of what someone in favour/against veganism might say: *on protège la planète, les animaux ont le droit de vivre.*

| 1 | 7 | | [1 mark] |

| 1 | 8 | | [1 mark] |

| 1 | 9 | | [1 mark] |

| 2 | 0 | | [1 mark] |

School life in Britain and in France

Listen to a British student and a French student comparing their school experience. Complete the sentences in **English**.

Answer all parts of the question.

2 1 . 1 The first aspect of school life that the students discuss concerns

_____.

[1 mark]

2 1 . 2 In France, if you have not made enough progress by the end of the school year,

you _____.

[1 mark]

2 1 . 3 School holidays are shorter in _____.

[1 mark]

> When hearing unfamiliar language, e.g. *redoubler*, try to work out the meaning with the help of context.

School rules

Listen to a French teacher explaining the importance of school rules to his students.

Complete the sentences by choosing the correct answer. Write the correct letter in the box.

- Do not rule out any option before you hear the recording.
- Try to discard one of the options (A, B, C) after hearing the recording once.
- Focus on the remaining two options as you listen for the second time.

Answer both parts of question 22.

`2 2 . 1` School rules are there to help …

A	people see reason.
B	promote good discipline.
C	those who lack discipline.

[ ] **[1 mark]**

`2 2 . 2` Failing to do homework …

A	is not normal.
B	is of little consequence.
C	will result in a detention.

[ ] **[1 mark]**

Answer both parts of question 23.

`2 3 . 1` Chatting in class …

A	prevents others from learning.
B	happens when pupils don't understand the lesson.
C	makes the teacher's job impossible.

[ ] **[1 mark]**

`2 3 . 2` Smoking in school is not allowed because schools …

A	must set a good example.
B	are also responsible for the physical wellbeing of pupils.
C	expect good behaviour at all times.

[ ] **[1 mark]**

My town

Listen to two Belgian students describing their towns to their exchange partners. Write down **one** advantage and **one** disadvantage for each town.

Complete the boxes in **English**.

> • While listening to the recording, try to identify words that indicate whether the speaker is explaining an advantage or a disadvantage, e.g. something they like or a problem they encounter.
> • If there is a word that you don't understand, e.g. *se garer*, try to draw conclusions from what you know. In this case use words like *voiture* and *impossible* to help you guess.

2 4		
	Advantage	**Disadvantage**

[2 marks]

2 5		
	Advantage	**Disadvantage**

[2 marks]

Social and environmental issues

While on holiday in France, you hear reports on social and environmental issues facing various French regions and towns.

For each report, choose the topic from the list and write the correct letter in the box.

A	pollution
B	climate change
C	poverty
D	racism
E	homelessness
F	rising sea levels
G	unemployment
H	global warming

Before you listen to the recording, think of at least one French word linked to each title (A to H). You can expect more than one clue in each report, but if you hear words you had thought of before listening to the recording, this will give you a head start.

2 6		**[1 mark]**

2 7		**[1 mark]**

2 8		**[1 mark]**

2 9		**[1 mark]**

A birthday party

Florence is talking about her birthday with her Swiss friend. Listen to their conversation.

Choose the correct answer to complete each sentence. Write the correct letter in the box.

> There are a few instances of negative forms in the conversation: *ne… pas* is used three times. The word *sans* (without) works like a negative form too, e.g. *sans grande importance* (without much importance, not very important). Being aware of negative forms will allow you to discard some possible answers, so make sure you know them.

Answer both parts of question 30.

| 3 | 0 | . | 1 |

Florence's birthday party …

A	went well.
B	was cancelled.
C	ended with her in hospital.

[1 mark]

| 3 | 0 | . | 2 |

When Florence's father suggested postponing her birthday celebration by a week, she …

A	thanked him.
B	agreed that her birthday is important.
C	said it was not worth the trouble.

[1 mark]

| 3 | 1 |

Florence's mother …

A	is back home.
B	is still in hospital.
C	has a broken leg.

[1 mark]

Section B   Questions and answers in **French**

Les études universitaires

Ecoutez Gabriel parler de son avenir avec son professeur principal.

3 2   Choisissez **deux** phrases qui sont vraies et écrivez les bonnes lettres dans les cases.

A	Tous les amis de Gabriel font leurs études à Montpellier.
B	Gabriel veut faire des études supérieures.
C	Il aimerait beaucoup vivre au bord de la mer.
D	Il va demander à ses copains s'il peut faire du covoiturage avec eux.

[2 marks]

3 3   Choisissez **deux** phrases qui sont vraies et écrivez les bonnes lettres dans les cases.

A	Gabriel pense que les études de médecine sont trop longues.
B	Pour devenir médecin, il faut avoir une licence de chimie.
C	Gabriel va probablement suivre les conseils de ses parents.
D	Il aimerait recevoir un salaire aussitôt que possible.

[2 marks]

- Remember that you are looking for statements that are true. For a statement to be true, there must not be any part of it that is false, e.g. 32 A – it is not all of Gabriel's friends who study in Montpellier but most of them, so the statement is false.
- Try not to guess what the answers are, e.g. 33 B – you might think that a degree in chemistry can lead to a career as a doctor, but that is not stated in the recording so you can't assume that it is a true statement.

Un échange scolaire

Ecoutez le directeur du collège Jean Giono accueillir des élèves qui participent à un échange scolaire.

> - Make sure you read the three questions closely. Careful reading of the instructions and situation will help you answer the first question.
> - Make sure you write your answers in French and do not include English words.

Complétez les phrases en **français**.

| 3 | 4 |.| 1 | Le directeur du collège s'adresse aux élèves _____.

[1 mark]

| 3 | 4 |.| 2 | Les participants à l'échange ainsi que les famillies d'accueil sont invités

_____.

[1 mark]

| 3 | 4 |.| 3 | Les journées libres sont _____ des familles d'accueil.

[1 mark]

3	5

Le bénévolat

Vous visitez une organisation caritative avec votre correspondant(e) français(e). Vous discutez avec un bénévole. Que fait-il pour aider?

Choisissez **trois** tâches auxquelles il participe et écrivez les bonnes lettres dans les cases.

A	servir les repas
B	changer les draps
C	collecter des dons
D	faire la vaisselle
E	faire des cartons à vêtements
F	faire les lits
G	préparer les repas
H	livrer les cartons alimentaires

- You have to identify three tasks that the volunteer takes part in. When listening to the recording, you will notice that all eight tasks are mentioned. Only the ones introduced by *je* are therefore relevant.
- Make sure you listen to the full recording, as some of the answers may be in the very last sentence.

☐ ☐ ☐

[3 marks]

END OF QUESTIONS

Answers and mark schemes

AQA GCSE French (9-1)

PRACTICE PAPER

H

Higher Tier Paper 2 Speaking

Time allowed: 10–12 minutes
(+12 minutes' supervised preparation time)

Candidate's material – Role-play and Photo card

Instructions

- During the preparation time you must prepare the Role-play card and Photo card given to you.
- You may make notes during the preparation time on the paper provided by your teacher-examiner. Do not write on the stimulus cards.
- Hand your notes and both stimulus cards to the teacher-examiner before the General Conversation.
- You must ask the teacher-examiner at least one question in the General Conversation.

Information

- The test will last a maximum of 12 minutes and will consist of a Role-play (approximately 2 minutes) and a Photo card (approximately 3 minutes), followed by a General Conversation (between 5 and 7 minutes) based on your nominated Theme and the remaining Theme which has not been covered in the Photo card.
- You must **not** use a dictionary at any time during the test. This includes the preparation time.

Teacher's scripts

Please note: The Practice Paper questions and answers have not been written or approved by AQA.

ROLE-PLAY 1

CANDIDATE'S ROLE

Instructions to candidates

Your teacher will play the part of your French friend and will speak first.

You should address your friend as *tu*.

When you see this – **!** – you will have to respond to something you have not prepared.

When you see this – **?** – you will have to ask a question.

Tu parles de ton nouveau copain/ta nouvelle copine à ton ami(e) français(e).

- Rencontre. Où et quand.

- Ce que vous avez en commun (**un** détail).

- Activités le weekend dernier (**deux** détails).

- **!**

- **?** Meilleur(e) ami(e)

- For the first bullet point, you could use the perfect tense e.g. *j'ai rencontré*.
- Use *on* or *nous* when referring to yourself and your friend.
- If you are using a verb to address the third bullet point, you will need to use the perfect tense e.g. *nous sommes allé(e)s/ nous avons fait …*
- Think about what the unexpected question might be, e.g. How well do you get on? How different are you? What do you look for in a friend? Have ideas ready for answers and listen carefully to the question asked.
- Ask your friend any question you want to about their best friend e.g. name, age, likes, dislikes, where he/she lives.

ROLE-PLAY 2

CANDIDATE'S ROLE

Instructions to candidates

Your teacher will play the part of the tourist office employee and will speak first.

You should address the tourist office employee as *vous*.

When you see this – **!** – you will have to respond to something you have not prepared.

When you see this – **?** – you will have to ask a question.

Vous parlez avec un(e) employé(e) de l'office de tourisme de Paris en France.

- Renseignements sur la ville.

- Visite – durée.

- **Deux** activités touristiques.

- **!**

- **?** Recommandation pour une activité pour les jeunes à Paris.

- Use *je voudrais* or *avez-vous* for the first bullet point. Ideally, ask for information plus something else, e.g. a map of the city.
- For the second bullet point, say something about the duration of your stay: you can give either the length of time or the dates.
- Mention two activities aimed at tourists for the third bullet point, e.g. *promenades en bateau-mouche, la tour Eiffel*.
- Think about what the unexpected question might be, e.g. What else interests you? Are you interested in …? Have ideas ready to answer these and listen carefully to the question asked.
- When you ask a question at the end, you could begin with *Pouvez-vous* + verb or *Avez-vous* + noun.

ROLE-PLAY 3

CANDIDATE'S ROLE

Instructions to candidates

Your teacher will play the part of your friend and will speak first.

You should address your friend as *tu*.

When you see this – **!** – you will have to respond to something you have not prepared.

When you see this – **?** – you will have to ask a question.

Tu parles de ta vie scolaire à ton ami(e) suisse.

- Ton collège (**un** détail).

- Journée scolaire (**deux** détails).

- Matière préférée et raison.

- **!**

- **?** Etudes l'année prochaine.

- Give a simple answer for the first bullet point, e.g. the size of the school, the number of pupils.
- Take care with the faux-ami *journée* (it does not relate to journeys!).
- State your favourite subject for the third bullet point and give a simple reason, e.g. you are good at it or you like the teacher.
- The unexpected question might refer to the past (e.g. asking what lessons you had yesterday), so you would need to use a verb in the perfect tense.
- Ask a question that includes a verb. It could be in the present tense, e.g. *Tu veux continuer tes études?*, or the immediate future, *Tu vas continuer…?*, or the future tense, *Tu continueras…?* or the conditional, e.g. *Tu voudrais continuer…?* Choose the option that suits you best.

Card A   **Candidate's Photo card**

- Look at the photo during the preparation period.

- Make any notes you wish to on an additional piece of paper.

- Your teacher will then ask you questions about the photo and about topics related to **free-time activities**.

Your teacher will ask you the following three questions and then **two more questions** which you have not prepared.

- Qu'est-ce qu'il y a sur la photo?

- Faire un barbecue, ça te plaît? Pourquoi?/pourquoi pas?

- Comment as-tu fêté ton dernier anniversaire?

- When describing the photo, start with phrases like *Au premier plan, À l'arrière-plan, À gauche/droite de la photo, il y a/on peut voir…*
- If you are asked for an opinion and a reason, make sure you give both to gain full marks.
- Look for clues about the time frame for your answer – the word *dernier* (last) in the third question indicates that you need to talk about the past.
- Think about what you might be asked for the two unexpected questions – you know it will be about free-time activities, but you know it won't be about your birthday.
- Make sure you answer in the correct time frame when asked a question about the future.

Card B   **Candidate's Photo card**

- Look at the photo during the preparation period.

- Make any notes you wish to on an additional piece of paper.

- Your teacher will ask you questions about the photo and about topics related to **travel and tourism**.

Your teacher will ask you the following three questions and then **two more questions** which you have not prepared.

- Qu'est-ce qu'il y a sur la photo?

- Qu'est-ce que c'est pour toi, des vacances idéales? … Pourquoi?

- Parle-moi des dernières vacances que tu as prises.

- As you know that the first question will always refer directly to the photo, try to think what extra details you could add in advance (weather, number of people, activities, physical descriptions).
- The second question asks what your ideal holidays are and why, so this is your chance to use a conditional, e.g. *j'aimerais…*, *je voudrais…*
- Use the perfect tense in response to the third question, about your last holiday, e.g. *je suis allé(e)…* and try to add extra details about what your holiday was like.
- The fourth (unprepared) question asks you to choose one option. After choosing it, give a reason for your choice, e.g. *Je préfère… parce que…*
- The fifth (unprepared) question tests your ability to talk about the future. Show that you can handle the future tense, e.g. *j'irai*, as well as the immediate future, e.g. *je vais aller*.

Card C   **Candidate's Photo card**

- Look at the photo during the preparation period.

- Make any notes you wish to on an additional piece of paper.

- Your teacher will ask you questions about the photo and about topics related to **current and future study and employment**.

Your teacher will ask you the following three questions and then **two more questions** which you have not prepared.

- Qu'est-ce qu'il y a sur la photo?

- Que penses-tu de ton collège?

- Quelles sont les matières que tu as aimées et que tu n'as pas aimées cette année? Pourquoi?

- To access higher marks, you must give and explain an opinion (as requested in the second question), so practise using *car* or *parce que* to do this.
- Look closely at the question and the tense of the verb: the third question asks what you liked and didn't like, rather than what you like now. Try to have a bank of negative adjectives available to you (e.g. *ennuyeux*, *barbant*, *nul*, *difficile*) for giving negative responses.
- The fourth (unprepared) question asks about your plans for future education: take note of the tense being used here. Use phrases like *j'espère*, *je voudrais*, *j'aimerais* followed by a verb in the infinitive, and then, say why.
- In the fifth (unprepared) question, use the future tense to talk about your career, e.g. *Je serai infirmier/infirmière*. Develop your answer by saying why you would like to choose this career, e.g. *Pour moi, il est important de…*

GENERAL CONVERSATION

The Photo card is followed by a General Conversation. The first part of the conversation will be on a theme nominated by the candidate and the second part on the other theme not covered by the Photo card. The total time for the General Conversation will be between 5 and 7 minutes and a similar amount of time should be spent on each theme. Here is a reminder of the three themes:

- Identity and culture

- Local, national, international and global areas of interest

- Current and future study and employment

The following pages show two examples of the general conversation with accompanying commentary on how these conversations would be marked, followed by tasks.

Conversation 1: Themes 1 and 2

Passons à la conversation. Tu as choisi le thème numéro un. Parle-moi un peu de ta famille.
Dans ma famille, il y a cinq personnes, mon père, ma mère, mon frère, ma sœur et moi.

Tu t'entends bien avec tout le monde?
Je m'entends bien avec mes parents et mon frère.

Et avec ta sœur?
Je me dispute souvent avec ma sœur. A mon avis, elle est casse-pieds.

Vous vous disputez à propos de quoi?
La télé.

Comment ça?
On n'aime pas les mêmes émissions. Moi, j'aime les programmes de sport et elle, les documentaires.

Qu'est-ce que tu as regardé à la télé hier?
J'ai regardé un bon match de foot.

Et ce soir, il y a quelque chose qui t'intéresse à la télé?
Je regarderai des comédies. J'aime bien rigoler.

Parle-moi un peu de tes amis.
Mon meilleur ami s'appelle Luc. Il a seize ans. Il aime bien jouer au foot. Nous nous entendons très bien.

Tu le vois souvent?
Tous les jours, au collège. En plus, on reste en contact grâce aux réseaux sociaux.

Tu utilises souvent les réseaux sociaux?

Oui, c'est bien pour communiquer avec les autres et aussi pour se faire de nouveaux amis.

Est-ce qu'ils présentent des risques?

Oui, il faut parler seulement aux gens qu'on connaît. Sinon, ça peut être dangereux.

Ce weekend, qu'est-ce que tu vas faire?

D'abord, je ferai mes devoirs. Si j'ai le temps, je voudrais sortir avec mes amis.

Où ça?

En ville. J'adore faire du shopping avec mes amis.

Qu'est-ce que tu vas acheter?

Je ne sais pas.

Tu vas faire autre chose?

Dimanche, c'est l'anniversaire de Luc. Il a organisé une fête et a invité tous ses copains. On va bien s'amuser.

Tes parents te laissent sortir le soir?

Oui, mais je dois dire où je vais et je dois être de retour avant vingt-deux heures.

Tu trouves ça raisonnable?

Oui, en général, ce n'est pas un problème. Je leur téléphone et ils viennent me chercher en voiture.

Tu te sers beaucoup de ton portable?

J'y suis un peu accro. Je trouve mon portable très utile.

Pour quelles raisons?

Pour mes études par exemple. On peut faire des recherches sur Internet.

Ça, c'est bien. Changeons un peu de sujet. On va parler maintenant au sujet du thème numéro 2. Parle-moi de ta maison.

J'habite une petite maison au centre-ville. Dans ma maison, il y a trois chambres, une cuisine, un salon, une salle à manger et une salle de bains. Il y a une chambre pour mes parents, une chambre pour ma sœur et une chambre pour mon frère et moi.

Comment est ta chambre?

Petite. Il y a deux lits, une armoire et un petit bureau. Je n'aime pas partager ma chambre avec mon frère.

Et ta ville, qu'est-ce que tu en penses?

J'aime ma ville. C'est une grande ville au bord de la mer. C'est super.

Tu vas à la plage?

Oui, pour me faire bronzer et nager dans la mer.

Qu'est-ce que tu aimes faire en ville?
J'aime aller au cinéma avec mes copains.

Est-ce qu'il y a des problèmes dans ta ville?
Oui, la pollution de l'air.

C'est à cause de l'industrie?
Non, il n'y a pas beaucoup d'industries ici.

C'est à cause de quoi alors?
La circulation. Il y a trop de voitures.

Il y a des solutions à ce problème?
Les gens doivent utiliser les transports en commun plus souvent.

Toi, tu les utilises beaucoup?
Non. En général, je me déplace à pied ou à vélo.

Que fais-tu d'autre pour protéger l'environnement?
Tous les weekends, je vais au centre de recyclage tous les weekends avec mon père. On recycle le papier, le carton et les bouteilles.

Est-ce qu'il y a des problèmes sociaux dans ta ville?
Oui, il y a des sans-abri qui passent la nuit dans les rues.

C'est parce qu'ils sont pauvres, je suppose?
Oui, ils n'ont pas de travail.

Comment peut-on aider ces gens?
On peut leur donner de l'argent.

Bien sûr. C'est tout?
On peut aussi faire du bénévolat.

Toi, tu fais du bénévolat?
Non. Et vous, vous faites du bénévolat?

Oui, pendant les vacances scolaires. Très bien. Merci.

Marks and commentary

	Communication	Range and accuracy of language	Pronunciation and intonation	Spontaneity and fluency	Total
Marks	4/10	5/10	3/5	3/5	**15/30**

This performance has been awarded 4 marks for communication, as answers tend not to have been developed. You can develop an answer by adding an extra detail, by giving an opinion and justifying it or by giving reasons for a statement. An opinion is given on at least seven occasions but only one is explained.

The teacher-examiner isn't asked a question until the very end of the conversation. This is risky because the conversation is meant to last between 5 and 7 minutes. What happens after 7 minutes does not count and cannot be credited.

5 marks were awarded for range and accuracy of language. In order to show a good range of language, it is best to avoid using certain phrases repeatedly. In this instance, *il y a*, *j'aime*, and *on peut* are used too often. There is however a reasonable range of language used. Three time frames have been included (past, present and future), as well as the conditional, irregular verbs, reflexive verbs and object pronouns.

With regards to pronunciation and intonation, we have assumed a reasonable performance and awarded 3 marks.

As far as spontaneity is concerned, there is little evidence that a lot of pre-learned material is being delivered (although possibly when the house is described). As for fluency, we have assumed that the performance is of a reasonably good standard, i.e. that there may well be some hesitations but that the conversation proceeds at a reasonable pace, so the mark given for spontaneity and fluency is 3.

> 1. **What is the French for the following linking words:** but; and; because.
>
> 2. **Answer the following questions, improving upon the responses given by using as many linking words as you can:**
>   - Parle-moi un peu de tes amis.
>   - Et ta ville, qu'est-ce que tu en penses?
>   - Que fais-tu d'autre pour protéger l'environnement?

Conversation 2: Themes 1 and 2

Passons à la conversation. Tu as choisi le thème numéro un. Parlons un peu de ta famille. Dis-moi, tu as de bons rapports avec ta famille?
Je m'entends bien avec mon petit frère et ma grande sœur mais je dois dire que, de temps en temps, je me dispute avec mes parents.

A propos de quoi?
En général, c'est quand je demande la permission de sortir le soir. Le weekend dernier par exemple, je voulais aller au cinéma avec mes copains mais mon père ne m'a pas laissé sortir. Evidemment, je me suis fâché contre lui.

Tes copains, on peut leur faire confiance?
Bien sûr. Ils sont super sympa. Mon meilleur ami a le même âge que moi et on a les mêmes idées. Comme moi, il est sérieux et travailleur mais il aime bien rigoler aussi.

Alors, qu'est-ce que tu as fait samedi soir?
Je suis monté dans ma chambre et j'ai passé la soirée devant mon ordinateur. Je me sers beaucoup des réseaux sociaux.

Tu ne trouves pas que les réseaux sociaux présentent des dangers?

Ils ont beaucoup plus d'avantages que d'inconvénients. Il est vrai qu'il y a des risques tels que le vol d'identité. Il faut aussi faire attention à ne pas parler aux gens qu'on ne connaît pas. Moi, je fais très attention.

Tu utilises les réseaux sociaux pour quelles raisons?

J'aime bien communiquer avec mes amis et partager mes photos et mes vidéos. A mon avis, il est important de rester en contact avec ses amis régulièrement. Et vous, utilisez-vous les réseaux sociaux?

Oui, bien sûr, mais pas souvent. Dis-moi, le weekend prochain, qu'est-ce que tu as l'intention de faire?

Samedi, j'irai à la piscine avec mon frère. Il adore la natation. Moi, j'en fais pour lui faire plaisir. L'après-midi, je jouerai au foot avec mon équipe. C'est en fait le sport que je préfère.

Et dimanche?

Je n'ai pas encore décidé. Je resterai probablement chez moi parce que j'ai beaucoup de devoirs en ce moment. Ce que j'aimerais, ce serait aller faire un tour en ville avec mes copains. On verra.

Qu'est-ce qu'il y a d'intéressant à faire en ville le dimanche?

La plupart des magasins sont ouverts. A part ça, on peut aussi aller à la patinoire ou voir un film au cinéma.

Bon, je te souhaite un bon weekend. Changeons un peu de sujet. On va parler maintenant au sujet du thème numéro 2. Parle-moi de ta maison.

J'habite dans une petite maison près du centre-ville. Au rez-de-chaussée, il y a le salon, la salle à manger et la cuisine. Au premier étage, on a trois chambres et une salle de bains. On n'a pas de jardin.

Comment est ta chambre?

A mon avis, trop petite. Je la partage avec mon frère qui est quelquefois assez pénible. J'aimerais avoir ma propre chambre.

Et ta ville, qu'est-ce que tu en penses?

Je la trouve bien. Au niveau des loisirs pour les jeunes, on a tout ce qu'il faut.

Est-ce qu'il y a des problèmes environnementaux dans ta ville?

Comme dans toutes les villes, la pollution de l'air est un grave problème. Il y a trop de circulation, surtout aux heures de pointe.

Il y a aussi des problèmes sociaux?

On voit des gens qui dorment sur les trottoirs en ville. Le nombre de sans-abri continue d'augmenter. C'est pareil pour le chômage. Il y a de plus en plus de personnes sans emploi. La pauvreté est devenue un problème important ici. On s'en rend compte quand on voit les gens faire la queue aux Restos du Cœur.

C'est quoi, les Restos du Cœur?

C'est un endroit où les gens qui n'ont pas d'argent peuvent manger gratuitement.

Qu'est-ce qu'on peut faire pour aider ces personnes?

Personnellement, tous les samedis, je fais du bénévolat. Je travaille aux Restos du Cœur de neuf heures à dix-sept heures. J'aide à servir les repas chauds qu'on offre aux gens et je fais aussi la vaisselle.

Bravo. Et en ce qui concerne l'environnement, que fais-tu pour le protéger?

Si c'est vraiment nécessaire, j'utilise les transports en commun. Sinon, je me déplace soit à pied soit à vélo. Chez nous, on recycle tout ce qui peut être recyclé comme par exemple le carton ou le verre. Je trouve que chacun doit faire son possible pour contribuer à une solution durable aux problèmes de l'environnement.

Je suis bien d'accord avec toi. A l'avenir, quelle sera ta contribution?

Quand j'aurai fini mes examens, j'irai travailler dans le centre de recyclage qui est près de chez moi.

Félicitations!

Marks and commentary

	Communication	Range and accuracy of language	Pronunciation and intonation	Spontaneity and fluency	Total
Marks	10/10	10/10	5/5	5/5	30/30

The full 10 marks for communication have been awarded, as well developed answers are given to each question. Communication is clear and effective. There are many opinions, a lot of which are explained.

10 marks have been awarded for range of language and accuracy as a very good variety of linguistic structures has been used, including three time frames. The following are included: perfect tense, imperfect tense, future tense, conditional, reflexive verbs, irregular verbs, object pronouns, negatives, a verb that follows another verb, a verb followed by *à* or *de*, comparatives, relative pronouns, link words, opinions, and justifications of opinion. The teacher-examiner has also been asked a question.

An excellent performance has been assumed with regards to pronunciation and intonation, with 5 marks awarded.

There is little evidence that pre-learned material is being delivered and all questions are responded to promptly. We can also assume that the conversation proceeds at a good pace, so full marks for spontaneity and fluency would be awarded.

1. **In the conversation, find examples of the following:**

    -   the perfect tense

    -   the imperfect tense

    -   the future tense

    -   the conditional

2. **Answer the following questions yourself, developing your answers as much as possible:**

    -   Alors, qu'est-ce que tu as fait samedi soir?

    -   Dis-moi, le weekend prochain, qu'est-ce que tu as l'intention de faire?

    -   A l'avenir, quelle sera ta contribution pour protéger l'environnement?

Model answers and mark schemes

AQA GCSE French (9-1)

Higher Tier Paper 3 Reading

Time allowed: 1 hour

Instructions

- Answer **all** questions.
- Answer the questions in the spaces provided.
- In **Section A**, answer the questions in **English**. In **Section B**, answer the questions in **French**. In **Section C**, translate the passage into **English**.
- Cross through any work you do not want to be marked.

Information

- The marks for the questions are shown in brackets.
- The maximum mark for this paper is 60.
- You must **not** use a dictionary.

Please note: The Practice Paper questions and answers have not been written or approved by AQA.

Section A Questions and answers in **English**

| 0 | 1 | **A healthy life**

Read these tips about how to stay healthy.

Which **four** pieces of advice are most appropriate for someone who is always tired and never takes any exercise?

Write the correct letters in the boxes.

Quelques conseils pour rester en bonne forme
A Suivez un régime alimentaire équilibré.
B Abstenez-vous de fumer.
C Dormez huit heures par nuit. Ne vous couchez pas trop tard.
D Pratiquez régulièrement un sport. Inscrivez-vous à un club.
E Ne vous droguez pas. Les drogues sont toutes très dangereuses.
F Ne consommez pas trop d'alcool.
G Faites de la marche plusieurs fois par semaine.
H Si vos circonstances vous le permettent, faites la grasse matinée le weekend.

> - Look out for words that relate to physical exercise or tiredness, e.g. *le sport*, *la fatigue*.
> - There are possible answers that are easy to discard as the sentences include near-cognates such as *alcool* and *drogues*.

☐ ☐ ☐ ☐

[4 marks]

0	2		**Job offers**

You read these job advertisements in a French local newspaper.

A On recherche un maçon qualifié. Disponible dès septembre.	**E** Jardinier pour propriété privée. Temps plein.
B Cherchons électricien ayant plusieurs années d'expérience.	**F** Infirmière à domicile. Doit avoir son propre moyen de transport. Bon salaire.
C Facteur temporaire pour la banlieue sud. Heures de travail: de 6 heures à 14 heures.	**G** Instituteur remplaçant pour le deuxième trimestre de l'année scolaire.
D Apprenti boulanger. Salaire minimum garanti.	**H** Secrétaire à temps partiel. Heures de travail négociables.

Which position would these people apply for? Write the correct letter in the box.

Read the eight job offers carefully. Try to identify the position on offer each time, then read questions 02.1–02.4 and link each statement with a job.

0	2	.	1	Someone who wants to look after the sick.		**[1 mark]**

0	2	.	2	Someone who would like to start a career in teaching.		**[1 mark]**

0	2	.	3	Someone who wishes to have a part-time job in an office.		**[1 mark]**

0	2	.	4	Someone who would enjoy delivering letters and parcels.		**[1 mark]**

0 3   **Helping those in need**

While in France, you pick up this invitation to take part in the activities of a charity.

> There are two clues in the text to help you answer question 03.1:
> *les sans-abri; ceux qui dorment dans la rue.*

Si nous sollicitons votre soutien pour les sans-abri de notre ville, c'est que nous n'avons pas les moyens suffisants pour le faire nous-mêmes. Nous vous demandons donc de faire des dons d'argent et de nourriture, de préférence d'une manière régulière.

Offrir un toit pour la nuit à ceux qui dorment dans la rue et s'assurer qu'ils n'ont pas l'estomac vide sont les buts principaux de notre association.

Si vous le souhaitez, vous pouvez aussi devenir membre de notre association et ainsi aider à distribuer les colis alimentaires, par exemple.

Nous vous remercions d'avance de votre contribution à notre cause.

Write the correct letter in each box.

0 3 . 1   This charity focuses on the needs of …

A	unemployed people.
B	poor people.
C	homeless people.

[1 mark]

0 3 . 2   You are asked to …

A	collect money.
B	give money.
C	collect food.

[1 mark]

0 3 . 3   One of the aims of the charity is to …

A	distribute money to those in need.
B	prepare food parcels.
C	feed those who do not have enough food.

[1 mark]

0 3 . 4   The charity also invites the reader to …

A	become a member.
B	ask others to contribute to its work.
C	advertise its work among their friends.

[1 mark]

| 0 | 4 | **Social media**

You read Manon's contribution to a French forum on the use of social media.

> **Manon**
> Les réseaux sociaux jouent un rôle important dans ma vie. Quand j'étais plus jeune, je m'en servais surtout pour me faire de nouvelles copines, mais maintenant c'est une manière pour moi d'exprimer mes idées et aussi de lire celles des autres.
>
> A mon avis, c'est en écoutant ce que les autres ont à dire qu'on forge ses propres opinions. C'est bien pour cela que je suis contente qu'il y ait des forums de discussion sur tous les sujets imaginables.
>
> Il est possible aussi qu'à l'avenir, grâce aux réseaux sociaux, je rencontre l'amour de ma vie. On n'est plus limités aux gens qu'on connait déjà. Pour moi, les réseaux sociaux sont un mécanisme qui nous permet d'ouvrir toutes sortes de portes qui étaient jusqu'à présent fermées.

- Try to spot the French phrases that match the beginning of the five questions. The answers to the questions are likely to be close by.
- Make sure that the sentences you have completed in English make sense.

Complete the sentences in **English**.

| 0 | 4 | . | 1 | When she was younger, Manon used social media to _____.

[1 mark]

| 0 | 4 | . | 2 | Nowadays, she is more interested in _____.

[1 mark]

| 0 | 4 | . | 3 | Manon believes social media helps you form _____.

[1 mark]

| 0 | 4 | . | 4 | In the future, thanks to social media, she hopes to _____.

[1 mark]

| 0 | 4 | . | 5 | She uses social media as it opens doors which _____.

[1 mark]

| 0 | 5 | | **Apprenticeships** |

You are in France at your exchange partner's school. You see this advertisement for apprenticeships on the school's information board.

> • Souhaitez-vous une qualification professionnelle, qui vous donnera un accès facile à l'emploi plus tard?
>
> • Voulez-vous gagner de l'argent dès que possible?
>
> Si votre réponse à ces deux questions est «oui», contactez-nous.
>
> Nous offrons des contrats d'apprentissage de deux ans. Votre formation se fera dans les bâtiments de l'université. Trois jours de la semaine y seront consacrés. Nous vous trouverons aussi une place dans une entreprise qui s'occupera de votre immersion professionnelle. Vous y passerez également trois jours par semaine. Evidemment, le dimanche est une journée libre pour tous.
>
> Votre travail dans cette entreprise sera rémunérée. Au bout de vos deux années d'apprentissage, vous recevrez un diplôme que vous pourrez présenter lorsque vous ferez une demande d'emploi.
>
> N'hésitez pas à nous demander des renseignements supplémentaires si l'apprentissage est la route que vous désirez suivre.

When answering questions in English, avoid single word answers as they are unlikely to answer the question fully. Equally, make sure your sentences are not too long, as they could add unnecessary information and lead to ambiguity.

Answer the questions in **English**.

| 0 | 5 | . | 1 | | What are the **two** main advantages of an apprenticeship, mentioned in the opening questions?

_____

_____

[2 marks]

▶ **Continued**

| 0 | 5 | . | 2 | What does an apprentice do each week?

_____

[1 mark]

| 0 | 5 | . | 3 | What happens after two years of apprenticeship?

_____

[1 mark]

| 0 | 5 | . | 4 | How would you find out whether the scheme covers a speciality that interests you?

_____

[1 mark]

| 0 | 6 | **A review of a package holiday**

You read this review of a package holiday.

> Ce n'est pas un voyage organisé que je recommanderais, ça, c'est certain. En plus, on n'a pas vraiment eu beau temps. Dès le départ, on a eu des problèmes. A cause de la grève des hôtesses de l'air, le vol a eu trois heures de retard et nous sommes arrivés à notre destination tard le soir. Notre chambre d'hôtel était au troisième étage et il n'y avait pas d'ascenseur. Cependant, la vue sur la mer était belle, il faut bien l'avouer.
>
> A l'hôtel, les repas étaient copieux et délicieux mais les serveurs n'étaient pas toujours agréables. Les excursions qu'on a faites en car étaient dans l'ensemble intéressantes, mais il n'y avait pas de climatisation et tout le monde avait trop chaud.
>
> On n'a pas payé un prix fou pour ce voyage, heureusement. J'aurais préféré payer un peu plus et avoir plus de confort. Je me le rappellerai avant de faire une réservation pour un autre voyage.

- Make sure you take note of the negatives in the text. They have to be noticed in order to answer most of these questions correctly.
- When you come across a word you think is needed to answer a question and you don't know what it means, e.g. *climatisation*, don't give up! There is often another clue nearby to help you get to that answer, e.g. *tout le monde avait trop chaud*.

Answer the questions in **English**.

| 0 | 6 | . | 1 | What was the weather like during their holiday?

_____

[1 mark]

| 0 | 6 | . | 2 | What caused the plane to be delayed?

_____

[1 mark]

| 0 | 6 | . | 3 | What was wrong with their hotel room?

_____

[1 mark]

▶ **Continued**

0 6 . 4   What didn't they like about the time spent on the coach?

_____

[1 mark]

0 6 . 5   What will they remember to do when booking another holiday?

_____

[1 mark]

0	7

Description of a town

While on holiday in France, you read this leaflet about the town of Evian-les-Bains.

Evian-les-Bains

Une destination de vacances idéale pour tous, jeunes et moins jeunes. Une ville riche en histoire située au bord du lac Léman. Célèbre pour son eau minérale, elle offre à ses visiteurs un accès facile à la montagne mais aussi à la Suisse qu'on peut voir du port ou de la plage par exemple.

Elle attire les fans de randonnées et de sports nautiques ainsi que ceux qui préfèrent le calme d'un terrain de golf ou une visite au théâtre.

Le funiculaire vous donne une perspective aérienne de la ville. Du sommet de la colline, vous profiterez de vues spectaculaires de la région.

Nous vous promettons un séjour inoubliable. Dès aujourd'hui réservez votre place dans un de nos hôtels grand confort. Vous ne le regretterez pas!

Bénéficiez de vingt pour cent de réduction sur le prix d'un séjour d'une semaine au mois de septembre.

- Although in most cases, the statements are listed in the order they can be found in the text, it is not always the case.
- Some answers are not stated explicitly in the text. Here, when you have understood that Evian-les-Bains is by a lake and that you can see Switzerland from the beach, you can deduce that Switzerland is a boat ride away.

Which **two** statements are true? Write the correct letters in the boxes.

A	Evian-les-Bains is the ideal holiday destination, mainly for young people.
B	Switzerland is only a boat ride away.
C	You can water ski in Evian-les-Bains.
D	A one-week holiday in Evian-les-Bains costs 20 per cent more if taken in September.

[2 marks]

0	8

Personal relationships

Read this extract from the novel '*Bonjour tristesse*' by Francoise Sagan, in which the narrator writes about a summer spent with her father.

- Read the extract to get the gist of it. Then read statements A to H and try to find where the answers are.
- Make sure you identify four true statements only. Offering more than four answers would invalidate all your answers.

Cet été-là, j'avais dix-sept ans et j'étais parfaitement heureuse. Les 'autres' étaient mon père et Elsa, sa maîtresse. Il me faut tout de suite expliquer cette situation qui peut paraître fausse. Mon père avait quarante ans, il était veuf depuis quinze; c'était un homme jeune, plein de vitalité, de possibilités, et, à ma sortie de pension, deux ans plus tôt, je n'avais pas pu ne pas comprendre qu'il vécut avec une femme. J'avais moins vite admis qu'il en changeât tous les six mois! Mais bientôt sa séduction, cette vie nouvelle et facile, mes dispositions m'y amenèrent.

C'était un homme léger, habile en affaires, toujours curieux et vite lassé, et qui plaisait aux femmes. Je n'eus aucun mal à l'aimer, et tendrement, car il était bon, généreux, gai, et plein d'affection pour moi. Je n'imagine pas de meilleur ami ni de plus distrayant. A ce début d'été, il poussa même la gentillesse jusqu'à me demander si la compagnie d'Elsa, sa maîtresse actuelle, ne m'ennuierait pas pendant les vacances.

Which **four** statements are true? Write the correct letters in the boxes.

A	The narrator, Cécile, is 17 years old.
B	Her father is married to Elsa.
C	He lost his first wife when he was 25 years old.
D	Two years ago, Cécile's father lived on his own.
E	Cécile was shocked by her father's affairs with women.
F	She loves her father and sees him as a friend.
G	Her father prefers the company of Elsa to that of Cécile.
H	At Cécile's request, all three characters are going on a holiday together.

[ ] [ ] [ ] [ ]

[4 marks]

Section B Questions and answers in **French**

0 9   **La poésie de Jacques Prévert**

Lisez ce poème de Jacques Prévert, *'Déjeuner du matin'.*

Déjeuner du matin

Il a mis le café

Dans la tasse

Il a mis le lait

Dans la tasse de café

Il a mis le sucre

Dans le café au lait

Avec la petite cuiller

Il a tourné

Il a bu le café au lait

Et il a reposé la tasse

Sans me parler

Il a allumé

Une cigarette

Il a fait des ronds

Avec la fumée

Il a mis les cendres

Dans le cendrier

Sans me parler

Sans me regarder

Il s'est levé

Il a mis

Son chapeau sur sa tête

- Take care with words that have more than one meaning. *Café* throughout this poem is used as meaning 'coffee', not a café i.e. a place.
- There are two words that will help you decide on the weather on that day. Understanding the word *sans* is the key to question 09.4.
- There are two clues in the last two lines that will help you work out the answer to question 09.5.

▶ **Continued**

> Il a mis
>
> Son manteau de pluie
>
> Parce qu'il pleuvait
>
> Et il est parti
>
> Sous la pluie
>
> Sans une parole
>
> Sans me regarder
>
> Et moi, j'ai pris
>
> Ma tête dans ma main
>
> Et j'ai pleuré.

Décidez si les phrases sont vraies (**V**), fausses (**F**) ou pas mentionnées (**PM**).

Ecrivez **V**, **F** ou **PM**.

0 9 . 1 La personne dont le poète parle a pris son café.   **[1 mark]**

0 9 . 2 Le poète prend son petit déjeuner à la terrasse d'un café.   **[1 mark]**

0 9 . 3 Il faisait beau ce jour-là.   **[1 mark]**

0 9 . 4 La conversation entre le poète et l'autre personne est brève.   **[1 mark]**

0 9 . 5 La fin du poème nous fait comprendre que c'est un poème triste.   **[1 mark]**

| 1 | 0 | **Améliorer son école** |

Lisez les suggestions des élèves de quatrième pour améliorer leur école.

Louis
Je pense qu'il faudrait abolir les retenues. En tout cas, je ne crois pas que cela décourage la mauvaise conduite.

Marie
Moi, je pense qu'on devrait pouvoir se servir de son portable en classe, parce que cela peut être vraiment utile.

Charlotte
J'aimerais qu'on nous donne moins de travail à compléter à la maison. Je n'ai presque pas de temps libre pour faire autre chose.

Jean-Laurent
On est ici entre huit heures et seize heures. A mon avis, c'est trop long.

- Look for synonyms between the two lists, e.g. *portable – téléphone*. This approach should help you with question 10.2.
- Look for words that have been paraphrased, e.g. homework in 10.3.

A quels aspects du règlement scolaire se réfèrent-ils?
Pour chaque personne, écrivez la bonne lettre dans la case.

A	Les absences
B	L'utilisations des téléphones
C	Le maquillage et les bijoux
D	La journée scolaire
E	Les examens
F	Les devoirs
G	Le système de punitions
H	L'uniforme scolaire

| 1 | 0 | . | 1 | Louis | | **[1 mark]** |

| 1 | 0 | . | 2 | Marie | | **[1 mark]** |

| 1 | 0 | . | 3 | Charlotte | | **[1 mark]** |

| 1 | 0 | . | 4 | Jean-Laurent | | **[1 mark]** |

1 1 **Les inégalités**

Vous êtes chez votre ami(e) belge. Ensemble, vous lisez cette contribution à un forum sur l'égalité des sexes.

Du temps de nos arrière-grands-parents, l'égalité des sexes n'était pas un principe dont beaucoup se souciaient. Dans beaucoup de familles, l'homme allait à son travail tandis que la femme s'occupait de la maison et élevait les enfants. De nos jours, ce n'est plus la même chose. La plupart des hommes contribuent aux tâches ménagères et beaucoup de femmes ont un travail en dehors de la maison. Nous n'en sommes certes pas arrivés à l'égalité totale mais c'est malgré tout devenu un but dans notre société. La discrimination sexuelle est peu à peu en train de disparaître. Espérons que les générations suivantes continueront dans cette voie et amélioreront ainsi la qualité de vie des femmes.

> - Some answers don't need full sentences, e.g. Who does the housework these days? 'Most men and women' works perfectly well as an answer.
> - As a general rule, you should keep your answer brief and simple, while ensuring that you have answered the question clearly.

Répondez aux questions en **français**.

1 1 . 1 Quel était le rôle des femmes auparavant? **Deux** détails.

_____

_____

[2 marks]

1 1 . 2 De nos jours, qui fait les tâches ménagères?

_____

[1 mark]

1 1 . 3 Si les générations suivantes continuent de combattre la discrimination sexuelle, qu'est-ce qui va changer pour les femmes?

_____

[1 mark]

1 2 **Sauver la planète**

Lisez cet article paru dans un magazine français sur la manière dont nous pouvons tous contribuer à sauver notre planète.

> Try to discard one of the three options (A, B, C) for each question. Take question 12.1: you are looking for a recommendation, so, clearly, option B is not right. You are now left with only two options. Make sure you understand the difference between them. Look for evidence in the text for option 1, then for option 2. Proceed in the same way for all five questions.

Pour sauver notre planète, mangeons moins de viande et plus de plantes et de graines! C'est le message qu'un groupe de scientifiques vient de nous envoyer. Plus les gens sont riches, plus ils mangent de viande. L'homme, semble-t-il, a un gros appétit pour la viande de bœuf en particulier, ce qui est devenu un problème environnemental. En plus, on a besoin de beaucoup d'espace pour élever ces animaux. Pour cela, on détruit des forêts pour les transformer en prés et en pâturages. Nous savons tous que les arbres absorbent d'énormes quantités de gaz carbonique. Ce gaz, ainsi que le méthane que les vaches et les bœufs émettent, contribuent à l'accélération du réchauffement climatique qui est devenu un problème mondial.

Alors que faire? La solution est simple, paraît-il – mangeons moins de viande! C'est aussi une manière de nous encourager à devenir végétariens ou végans. C'est peut-être ce que nous devons faire pour protéger notre planète et assurer la survie de l'humanité à long terme.

Complétez les phrases. Ecrivez la bonne lettre dans chaque case.

1 2 . 1 Un groupe de scientifiques nous recommande …

A	de ne pas manger de viande.
B	de faire passer leur message.
C	de manger moins de viande.

[1 mark]

1 2 . 2 Pour élever de plus en plus de bœufs et de vaches, il faut …

A	moins d'espace.
B	détruire des forêts.
C	des fermes spécialisées.

[1 mark]

▶ Continued

1 2 . 3 Les forêts …

A	absorbent le gaz carbonique.
B	absorbent le méthane.
C	sont un problème mondial.

[1 mark]

1 2 . 4 Les émissions de gaz contribuent …

A	à la couche d'ozone.
B	au réchauffement de la terre.
C	à la destruction des forêts.

[1 mark]

1 2 . 5 La meilleure solution est de …

A	manger de la viande.
B	devenir végétarien.
C	protéger l'humanité.

[1 mark]

Section C   Translation into **English**.

Your friend has seen this post on social media and asks you to translate it for him/her into **English**.

> On nous conseille toujours de faire du sport ou tout au moins de faire de l'exercice physique d'une manière régulière. Ces activités nous aideront à nous maintenir en bonne forme et auront des effets positifs sur notre santé. Pour mener une vie saine, il est essentiel de suivre ces conseils.

[9 marks]

- Check that what you have written in English makes sense and is grammatically correct.
- Take care with cognates and semi-cognates. Some translate easily, e.g. *sport, régulière, activités, effets, positives, essentiel*. Others do not, e.g. *conseille* (advise).
- Watch out for tenses. The present tense (*on nous conseille*) and the conditional (*aideraient, auraient*) are both used in the text. Use 'would …' to translate the conditional.

END OF QUESTIONS

Answers and mark schemes

PRACTICE PAPER

Higher Tier Paper 4 Writing

Time allowed: 1 hour 15 minutes

Instructions

- You must answer **three** questions.
- You must answer **either** Question 1.1 **or** Question 1.2. Do not answer both of these questions.
- You must answer **either** Question 2.1 **or** Question 2.2. Do not answer both of these questions.
- You must answer Question 3.
- Answer all questions in **French**.
- Answer the questions in the spaces provided.
- Cross through any work you do not want to be marked.

Information

- The marks for the questions are shown in brackets.
- The maximum mark for this paper is 60.
- You must **not** use a dictionary during this test.
- In order to score the highest marks for Question 1.1/Question 1.2, you must write something about each bullet point. You must use a variety of vocabulary and structures and include your opinions.
- In order to score the highest marks for Question 2.1/Question 2.2, you must write something about both bullet points. You must use a variety of vocabulary and structures and include your opinions and reasons.

Please note: The Practice Paper questions and answers have not been written or approved by AQA.

Answer **either** Question 1.1 **or** Question 1.2.
You must **not** answer **both** of these questions.

EITHER Question 1.1

| 0 | 1 | . | 1 | Vous décrivez votre famille pour votre blog.

Décrivez:

- chaque personne de votre famille

- avec qui vous vous entendez bien et pourquoi

- avec qui vous vous êtes disputé(e) récemment et pourquoi

- ce que vous allez faire en famille le weekend prochain.

Ecrivez environ **90** mots en **français**. Répondez à chaque aspect de la
question.   **[16 marks]**

> - In questions 1 and 2 of the Writing paper, the bullet points and form of address could be in the *tu* or *vous* form.
> - In this question there will always be one bullet point which refers to a past time frame and one which refers to a future time frame.
> - To say who you get on with, start with *Je m'entends bien…* and choose a reason that you can easily express in French.
> - Use the near future or future tense to describe what you are going to do, e.g. *Je vais sortir/Je sortirai…*

OR Question 1.2

| 0 | 1 | . | 2 | Vous décrivez les problèmes de l'environ-
nement dans votre ville à votre ami(e)
français(e).

Décrivez:

- le problème principal

- une solution possible à ce problème

- ce que vous avez fait récemment pour contribuer à une solution

- un autre problème environnemental dans votre ville que vous aimeriez résoudre à l'avenir.

> - Jot down a few words linked to environmental issues that you intend to use, e.g. *environnementaux, circulation, pollution, voitures, transports en commun.*
> - Don't forget to express an opinion – you don't always have to use *j'aime/je préfère/ je déteste*; you could start a sentence with *A mon avis.*
> - Make sure you talk about an environmental problem in your town (e.g. littering) for the last bullet point and not a global issue.

Ecrivez environ **90** mots en **français**. Répondez à chaque aspect de la question.   **[16 marks]**

Answer **either** Question 2.1 **or** Question 2.2.
You must **not** answer **both** of these questions.

EITHER Question 2.1

| 0 | 2 | . | 1 | Vous donnez des détails sur votre scolarité à votre ami(e) français(e).

Décrivez:

- votre vie scolaire

- les études que vous voulez faire à l'avenir.

> - Make sure you include opinions and justifications of opinions.
> - Use different time frames (present, past and future) where appropriate and other tenses if you can, e.g. the conditional *j'aimerais*.
> - Include object pronouns if appropriate, e.g. *Je l'aime beaucoup*.
> - Combine irregular verbs, negatives and object pronouns if you can, e.g. *Je ne peux pas le supporter*.

Ecrivez environ **150** mots en **français**. Répondez aux deux aspects de la question.

[32 marks]

OR Question 2.2

| 0 | 2 | . | 2 | Vous écrivez comment vous utilisez votre portable pour votre blog.

Décrivez:

- les raisons pour lesquelles vous utilisez votre portable

- les bienfaits et les dangers de la technologie mobile, maintenant et à l'avenir.

> - Plan your answer by making a list of the occasions when you use your phone, before moving on to the second part of the question and doing the same.
> - Try to avoid repetition of certain phrases such as *J'utilise*. Think of synonyms, like *Je me sers de* or a paraphrase: *Le téléphone me permet de…*
> - Make sure you include at least two opinions and justify those opinions, e.g. *Je pense que… parce que…*

Ecrivez environ **150** mots en **français**. Répondez aux deux aspects de la question.

[32 marks]

0 3   Translate the following passage into **French**.

> We usually go on holiday in August and spend two weeks by the sea. I like that very much because we live in town, which is a completely different way of life. Last year, we went to Cassis in the south of France. It was hot every day. We all had a good time.

[12 marks]

- If you don't know the vocabulary required, try a synonym, e.g. a way of life = *un mode de vie*, but *une façon/une manière de vivre*, while not perfect, would communicate the same meaning.
- The last three sentences require the use of the perfect tense, so make sure the auxiliary (*avoir* or être) is given its correct form, and the past participle agrees with the subject of the sentence if the auxiliary is *être*.
- Don't forget to include the correct reflexive pronoun when using a reflexive verb (in this case, *nous*).
- When you have finished, read your translation to check that it makes sense.

_____

_____

_____

_____

_____

_____

_____

_____

END OF QUESTIONS

Model answers and mark schemes

AQA GCSE French (9-1)

Higher Tier Paper 1 Listening

Time allowed: 45 minutes
(including 5 minutes' reading time before the test)

You will need no other materials.
The pauses are pre-recorded for this test.

Information
- The marks for the questions are shown in brackets. The maximum mark for this paper is 50.
- You must **not** use a dictionary.

Advice
This is what you should do for each item.
- After the question number is announced, there will be a pause to allow you to read the instructions and questions.
- Listen carefully to the recording and read the questions again.
- Listen to the recording again, and then answer the questions.
- When the next question is about to start you will hear a bleep.
- You may write at any time during the test.
- In **Section A**, answer the questions in **English**. In **Section B**, answer the questions in **French**.
- You must answer all the questions in the spaces provided. Do not write on blank pages.
- Write neatly and put down all the information you are asked to give.
- **You must not ask questions or interrupt during the test.**
- You have five minutes to read through the question paper. You may make notes during this time. You may turn to the questions now.
- **The test starts now.**

Listen to the audio

Please note: The Practice Paper questions and answers have not been written or approved by AQA.

Section A   Questions and answers in **English**

Moving house

Marie talks on the phone to her friend Luc, who has moved to a different town, about the consequences of moving house. Listen to their conversation.

0 1   Choose **two** sentences that are **true** and write the correct letters in the boxes.

A	Marie and Luc miss each other.
B	They say that when you move house, you find new friends.
C	For Luc, keeping in touch with friends by phone is the same as seeing them in person.
D	When you don't see friends in person, you lose contact with them.

[2 marks]

0 2   Choose **two** sentences that are **true** and write the correct letters in the boxes.

A	Marie and Luc did not like each other when they first met.
B	Marie and Luc plan to keep in touch in the long term.
C	Luc will meet Marie's new friends at Easter.
D	Marie will visit Luc at Easter.

[2 marks]

Enquiring about a holiday

You hear a French travel agent describing a package holiday to a customer.

> • Read the questions carefully. You will notice that you need a length of time (for question 03.1), the name of a country (03.2) and a total number of nights (03.5). Focus on these three aspects as you listen for the first time.
> • Focus on the remaining two questions (03.3 and 03.4) as you listen to the recording for the second time.
> • If after you have heard the recording for the second time, you don't know the answer to a particular question, don't leave a blank. Have an educated guess – it is worth a try!

Complete the sentences in **English**.

0 3 . 1 The holiday discussed lasts _____ .

[1 mark]

0 3 . 2 The journey takes customers to countries in the Mediterranean and

_____ .

[1 mark]

0 3 . 3 From any starting point in France, the price includes _____ to Marseille.

[1 mark]

0 3 . 4 Also included in the package are _____ and

_____ .

[2 marks]

0 3 . 5 In total, _____ nights are spent in hotels.

[1 mark]

A gap year

You hear four French students talking about the value of taking a gap year.

What kind of views do they express?

For a negative opinion, write **N**.

For a positive opinion, write **P**.

For a positive and negative opinion, write **P+N**.

0 4		[1 mark]

0 5		[1 mark]

0 6		[1 mark]

0 7		[1 mark]

Life as a couple

You hear four Belgians talking about the pros and cons of living with a partner.

What is each person's view of living together?

For a negative opinion, write **N**.

For a positive opinion, write **P**.

For a positive and negative opinion, write **P+N**.

Listen out for words such as *se marier*, *le mariage*, *le concubinage*, *vivre ensemble*, *célibataire*, *partenaire*. They are likely to be the key to each answer; but pay attention in case they are used with a negative phrase or expression.

0 8		[1 mark]

0 9		[1 mark]

1 0		[1 mark]

1 1		[1 mark]

Winning the lottery

You hear four people being interviewed on French radio about what they would do if they won the lottery.

Choose the correct answer to complete each sentence.

Write the correct letter in the box.

1 2 This player would …

A	spend all the money on herself.
B	see to the needs of her family and friends.
C	give her family and friends all the money they want.

[1 mark]

1 3 This winner would …

A	invest some money.
B	try to spend it all.
C	give most of it to his chosen charities.

[1 mark]

1 4 This person would …

A	buy a house.
B	travel round the world with her friends.
C	have a holiday by the sea.

[1 mark]

1 5 This speaker would give money to charities that support …

A	the homeless.
B	the local area.
C	the quality of the environment.

[1 mark]

A job interview

Listen to Adèle's job interview in Paris.

Answer the questions in **English**.

> - Listen carefully to Adèle's replies: listen out for a reason (16.1), a qualification (16.2), a strength (17.1), a weakness (17.2), an activity (18.1) and an ambition (18.2).
> - Check that the points listed are all present in your answers.

Answer both parts of question 16.

`1 6 . 1`   Why did Adèle apply for this particular job?

_____

[1 mark]

`1 6 . 2`   What qualifications does she have?

_____

[1 mark]

Answer both parts of question 17.

`1 7 . 1`   What is her main strength?

_____

[1 mark]

`1 7 . 2`   What weakness does she mention?

_____

[1 mark]

Answer both parts of question 18.

`1 8 . 1`   What does she like doing in her free time?

_____

[1 mark]

`1 8 . 2`   What ambition does she have in terms of her career?

_____

[1 mark]

Christmas celebrations

You hear four people on a French radio programme saying how they feel about Christmas celebrations. What are their views?

For a negative opinion, write **N**.

For a positive opinion, write **P**.

For a positive and negative opinion, write **P+N**.

| 1 9 | | [1 mark] |

| 2 0 | | [1 mark] |

| 2 1 | | [1 mark] |

| 2 2 | | [1 mark] |

Problems at school

You hear three French pupils talking about problems they face in school.

For each speaker, choose the correct problem.

Write the correct letter in the box.

A	exam pressure
B	homework
C	punctuality
D	behaviour in class
E	peer group pressure
F	bullying

Don't jump to conclusions too quickly when you hear a word like *devoirs*, for instance. It could indicate option B, or it could be being mentioned in a different context. If in doubt, make a note of what you think the answer might be and finalise your answers after hearing the recording for the second time.

| 2 3 | | [1 mark] |

| 2 4 | | [1 mark] |

| 2 5 | | [1 mark] |

A guided visit

You hear a French tour guide explaining the programme for the day's excursion to Orange, a town in the south of France.

Answer the questions in **English**.

Answer all parts of question 26.

| 2 | 6 |.| 1 | Where is the Arc de Triomphe situated?

_____

[1 mark]

| 2 | 6 |.| 2 | Where is the coach going to park?

_____

[1 mark]

| 2 | 6 |.| 3 | What must the visitors do at 11 o'clock?

_____

[1 mark]

Answer both parts of question 27.

| 2 | 7 |.| 1 | Where is the Théâtre Antique situated?

_____

[1 mark]

| 2 | 7 |.| 2 | Name one thing that the guide suggests visitors do after visiting the Théâtre Antique.

_____

[1 mark]

Section B   Questions and answers in **French**

Le weekend dernier

Ecoutez ces trois jeunes Français parler de ce qu'ils ont fait le weekend dernier.

Complétez les phrases en **français**.

> Notice that all three sentences end with *est allé(e)*. You can work out that the answers involve either a place or an activity.

| 2 | 8 | Dimanche dernier, Charlotte est allée _____. |

[1 mark]

| 2 | 9 | Henri est allé _____. |

[1 mark]

| 3 | 0 | Après être passée chez le coiffeur, Alice est allée _____. |

[1 mark]

Le mode de vie d'avant

Ecoutez ces trois Luxembourgeois parler du mode de vie du temps de leurs arrière-grands-parents.

Pour chaque personne, choisissez la phrase qui est **vraie**.

Ecrivez la bonne lettre dans chaque case.

A	On ne buvait pas d'alcool.
B	Les gens vivaient plus longtemps que de nos jours.
C	La majorité des gens n'avait pas beaucoup d'argent.
D	On ne mangeait pas sainement.
E	Il n'y avait pas beaucoup de circulation.
F	On faisait beaucoup de sport.

| 3 | 1 | ☐ |

[1 mark]

| 3 | 2 | ☐ |

[1 mark]

| 3 | 3 | ☐ |

[1 mark]

La pression des examens

Ecoutez ce conseiller d'orientation français parler aux élèves qui préparent leurs examens.

Décidez si les phrases sont vraies (**V**), fausses (**F**) ou pas mentionnées (**PM**).

Ecrivez **V**, **F** ou **PM**.

> Try to answer as many questions as you can the first time you listen. Focus on the remaining answers as you listen for the second time. If by then you have been unable to answer a particular question, it may well be because the information you needed has not been mentioned (NM).

3 4 . 1 L'école exerce une grosse pression sur les élèves qui se présentent aux examens.

[1 mark]

3 4 . 2 Les professeurs exercent cette pression pour les mêmes raisons que les parents.

[1 mark]

3 4 . 3 La pression des examens est intolérable pour certains élèves.

[1 mark]

3 4 . 4 Le conseiller pense que le mieux est de ne pas se soucier de cette pression.

[1 mark]

END OF QUESTIONS

Answers and mark schemes

AQA GCSE French (9-1)

Higher Tier Paper 2 Speaking

Time allowed: 10-12 minutes
(+12 minutes' supervised preparation time)

Candidate's material – Role-play and Photo card

Instructions

- During the preparation time you must prepare the Role-play card and Photo card given to you.
- You may make notes during the preparation time on the paper provided by your teacher-examiner. Do not write on the stimulus cards.
- Hand your notes and both stimulus cards to the teacher-examiner before the General Conversation.
- You must ask the teacher-examiner at least one question in the General Conversation.

Information

- The test will last a maximum of 12 minutes and will consist of a Role-play (approximately 2 minutes) and a Photo card (approximately 3 minutes), followed by a General Conversation (between 5 and 7 minutes) based on your nominated Theme and the remaining Theme which has not been covered in the Photo card.
- You must **not** use a dictionary at any time during the test. This includes the preparation time.

Teacher's scripts

Please note: The Practice Paper questions and answers have not been written or approved by AQA.

ROLE-PLAY 1

CANDIDATE'S ROLE

Instructions to candidates

Your teacher will play the part of your friend and will speak first.

You should address your friend as *tu*.

When you see this – **!** – you will have to respond to something you have not prepared.

When you see this – **?** – you will have to ask a question.

Tu parles d'un festival de musique récent à ton ami(e) luxembourgeois(e).

- Type de festival et quand.

- Transport et durée du trajet.

- Ce qu'il y avait d'intéressant (**deux** détails).

- **!**

- **?** Genre de festival préféré et une raison.

- Use the perfect tense of *aller* or *c'était…* to answer the first question. Note that you can say when it was without necessarily adding another verb, e.g. *Je suis allé(e) à un festival de musique pop la semaine dernière.*
- You could say how you got there without using a verb, e.g. *en voiture*. However, you will need a verb to say how long it took, e.g. *ça a pris…* Alternatively, you could combine the two into one phrase, e.g. *On a passé deux heures dans le train.*
- Use a verb in the perfect tense to talk about what you saw/heard/did, e.g. *J'ai vu/entendu/fait…*
- Think about what you could be asked for the unexpected question. It might be: Did you have a good time? Did you stay in a hotel? What was the best bit of the festival? Have ideas ready for these and listen carefully to the question the teacher asks.
- Ask what kind of festival your friend prefers, e.g. *Quel genre de festival préfères-tu? Quel est ton genre de festival préféré? Tu préfères quel genre de festival?*

ROLE-PLAY 2

CANDIDATE'S ROLE

Instructions to candidates

Your teacher will play the part of your friend and will speak first.

You should address your friend as *tu*.

When you see this – **!** – you will have to respond to something you have not prepared.

When you see this – **?** – you will have to ask a question.

Ta famille va déménager. Tu parles à ton ami(e) français(e) de ta nouvelle maison.

- Déménager – quand et où.

- Comment te contacter.

- Nouvelle maison (**deux** détails).

- **!**

- **?** Photos de la nouvelle maison.

- You don't have to use a verb to answer the question about when the move will take place. Use the immediate future or the future tense to say where you are moving to.
- Use the immediate future or the future tense to give your new details or explain that your phone number and email address will not change.
- Give two details about your new home, e.g. It is big. It has a large garden.
- For the unexpection question you will need to give your opinion (*j'aime…, je n'aime pas…*) about two different aspects of the house.
- Ask any question about photos of the new house, for example, ask if your friend would like to see some photos (*Tu voudrais…?*).

ROLE-PLAY 3

CANDIDATE'S ROLE

Instructions to candidates

Your teacher will play the part of the French teacher and will speak first.

You should address the French teacher as *vous*.

When you see this – **!** – you will have to respond to something you have not prepared.

When you see this – **?** – you will have to ask a question.

Vous parlez de l'échange scolaire auquel vous participez avec le professeur français qui en est responsable.

- Correspondant(e) français(e) (**un** détail).

- Opinion de l'école française (**deux** détails).

- Les avantages d'un échange scolaire (**deux** détails).

- **!**

- **?** Visite de retour.

- You could say what your exchange partner is like, with an adjective, or say something about the relationship, e.g. he/she is the same age as you, you have similar tastes, you get on well together.
- When asked about the French school, you could compare it to your school, or you could give your opinion of the pupils and the teachers you have met. Choose details you know you can express in good French.
- For the advantages of a school exchange, you could say that it helps people learn a language, that you like school trips, etc.
- Listen carefully to the unexpected question the teacher asks you. Notice that the question refers to the future (*vous allez continuer, vous quitterez*) so use the immediate future or the future tense in your response.
- Ask any suitable question you like about the return visit, e.g. When will it be? How long will it be? Use the correct intonation for a question.

Card A   **Candidate's Photo card**

- Look at the photo during the preparation period.

- Make any notes you wish to on an additional piece of paper.

- Your teacher will ask you questions about the photo and about topics related to **free-time activities**.

Your teacher will ask you the following three questions and then **two more questions** which you have not prepared.

- Qu'est-ce qu'il y a sur la photo?

- Tu penses que le sport est important? Pourquoi?

- Quel sport as-tu pratiqué récemment?

- Don't spend too long on the first question as you might run out of time: you could mention the number of people in the photo, where they are and what they are doing.
- To say why sport is important, you could mention health reasons (*pour garder la forme*) or social reasons (*pour se faire des amis*).
- You don't always have to tell the truth in your answers, so you could say you've done any kind of sport recently, as long as you communicate it correctly.
- The first unexpected question here refers to free-time activities, so think about what might be asked. Try to ensure you don't just give a yes or no answer to the question asked: in this case, you could use the conditional to talk about an extreme sport you'd like to try (*J'aimerais bien… parce que je pense que ce serait…*).
- The second unexpected question requires you to talk about something in the future, so make sure you use a future tense in your response, e.g. *je ferai*).

Card B   **Candidate's Photo card**

- Look at the photo during the preparation period.

- Make any notes you wish to on an additional piece of paper.

- Your teacher will ask you questions about the photo and about topics related to **social issues**.

Your teacher will ask you the following three questions and then **two more questions** which you have not prepared.

- Qu'est-ce qu'il y a sur la photo?

- Comment est-ce que les associations caritatives peuvent aider les pauvres, à ton avis?

- As-tu déjà fait du bénévolat?

- Think of extra details you could add (other than saying who is in the photo); maybe where it was taken, what people are carrying on their heads, what issues the photo raises or represents.
- To access higher mark bands, make sure you explain your opinion as well as giving it. As well as thinking about money (*collecter/envoyer de l'argent*), you could think about other resources that charities provide, such as volunteers.
- If it's easier for you to say, pretend you have done some voluntary work. You could use phrases such as *je n'ai pas le temps* or *il n'y a pas d'organisations caritatives là où j'habite* if you haven't done any voluntary work.
- For the first unexpected question, don't give a short answer, e.g. just *le chômage*. Explain what the situation is in as much detail as you can and the possible reasons for it.
- The last question asks you about something you would like to do in future, so your answer needs to be given in the conditional (*j'aimerais/je voudrais...*).

Card C   **Candidate's Photo card**

- Look at the photo during the preparation period.

- Make any notes you wish to on an additional piece of paper.

- Your teacher will ask you questions about the photo and about topics related to **jobs, career choices and ambitions**.

Your teacher will ask you the following three questions and then **two more questions** which you have not prepared.

- Qu'est-ce qu'il y a sur la photo?

- Parle-moi d'un entretien d'embauche que tu as passé.

- Comment doit-on se préparer pour un entretien d'embauche, à ton avis?

- Say where the photo was taken, e.g. *dans un bureau*, how many people there are, who they are and what they are doing. Use phrases like *un entretien d'embauche* and *poser des questions*.
- If you have had the experience of a job interview, you could say what happened, what questions you were asked, whether you were offered the job. If you have never had an interview, say why not, e.g. *Je suis encore au collège*.
- To gain marks in the top band you must give and explain an opinion. For example, you could explain why you feel that preparing for a job interview might be difficult in response to the third question, just in case you run out of time to give opinions later in the conversation.
- For the fourth (unprepared) question, try to mention at least two strengths and two weaknesses that you know you can express in French, e.g. reliable, punctual and honest. Don't forget to use verbs and add extra details, e.g. I find it difficult to get up early and I get tired in the afternoon.
- Make sure that you talk about the future in your final unprepared answer, e.g. use *je vais* + infinitive. Say what career tempts you and why (*Je voudrais devenir… parce que…*).

GENERAL CONVERSATION

The Photo card is followed by a General Conversation. The first part of the conversation will be on a theme nominated by the candidate and the second part on the other theme not covered by the Photo card. The total time for the General Conversation will be between 5 and 7 minutes and a similar amount of time should be spent on each theme. Here is a reminder of the three themes:

- Identity and culture

- Local, national, international and global areas of interest

- Current and future study and employment

The following pages show two examples of the general conversation with accompanying commentary on how these conversations would be marked, followed by tasks.

Conversation 1: Themes 1 and 3

Passons à la conversation. Tu as choisi le thème numéro un. Parle-moi de ta famille.
Dans ma famille, il y a ma sœur, ma mère et moi. Nous sommes une famille monoparentale.

Tu t'entends bien avec elles?
Oui, j'aime beaucoup ma sœur et ma mère.

Décris la caractère de ta sœur.
Elle est sympa. Elle aime bien rire. On s'entend bien.

Et physiquement?
Elle est plus petite que moi. Elle a seulement onze ans. Elle a les yeux verts et les cheveux bruns et longs.

Vous avez des animaux domestiques chez vous?
Oui, un chien. Il est gentil. Je le promène tous les jours.

Tu as beaucoup d'amis?
Oui.

Qu'est-ce que vous aimez faire ensemble?
On va au cinéma ou à la piscine.

Ce sont tes activités préférées?
Oui, j'aime regarder des films d'action et je suis sportive.

Qu'est-ce que tu pratiques comme sports?
La natation et l'athlétisme.

Tu fais ça où et quand?
Je vais à la piscine le weekend et je fais de l'athlétisme à l'école.

Tu as des cousins et des cousines?
J'ai un cousin qui habite près de chez nous.

Tu le vois souvent?
Non, parce que quand on se voit, on se dispute.

A propos de quoi?
De tout. Des garçons, de l'école, de la télé.

Avec qui est-ce que tu t'entends le mieux?
Ma meilleure amie s'appelle Hélène. Elle est super gentille.

Elle a le même âge que toi?
Oui, elle a seize ans. Son anniversaire est la semaine prochaine.

Comment allez-vous fêter ça?
Elle a organisé une fête d'anniversaire chez elle. Elle a invité vingt personnes.

Ça va être super, non?
Oui, je pense.

Tu lui as acheté un cadeau?
Pas encore. Je vais lui acheter un T-shirt.

C'est gentil, ça. Bonne fête d'anniversaire alors. Maintenant, passons au thème numéro 3. Parle-moi de ta vie scolaire.
J'aime mon école parce que j'y vois mes amis tous les jours mais je n'aime pas les devoirs.

C'est utile les devoirs, non?
Non.

Qu'est-ce que tu fais comme matières?
Les maths, l'anglais et les sciences. J'ai choisi d'étudier le français, l'histoire et la musique.

Quelle est ta matière préférée?
La musique. J'adore la musique.

Il y a une matière que tu n'aimes pas?
L'anglais. C'est ennuyeux.

Tu arrives au collège à quelle heure le matin?
A huit heures et demie. Le premier cours est à neuf heures.

Qu'est-ce que tu fais à la récréation?
En général, je parle avec mes amis.

Et pour la pause-déjeuner?
Je mange à la cantine.

Tu es de retour chez toi à quelle heure après l'école?
A quatre heures. Je rentre en bus parce que j'habite assez loin du collège.

L'année prochaine, tu vas continuer tes études?

Oui, j'irai au lycée où j'étudierai la musique et l'histoire.

Tu aimerais aller à l'université?

Oui, je voudrais être étudiant. J'aimerais avoir une licence de musique.

Tu ferais ça où?

Peut-être à Bristol. Ce serait bien parce que j'ai un copain qui habite à Bristol.

Et comme métier plus tard?

Je ne sais pas. Si je pouvais gagner ma vie comme musicien, ce serait parfait. Vous aimez votre métier de prof?

Oui, bien sûr. Nous avons fini maintenant. Je te souhaite bonne chance pour l'avenir.

Marks and commentary

	Communication	Range and accuracy of language	Pronunciation and intonation	Spontaneity and fluency	Total
Marks	4/10	5/10	3/5	3/5	**15/30**

This conversation is given 4 marks for communication as most answers are short and simple sentences, with only occasional extended responses. Hardly any details are added, although a simple opinion is often given and a question is asked late in the exchange which is risky. A couple of opinions are explained, e.g. why they like their school or why they would like to be a student in Bristol – but not frequently enough.

For range and accuracy of language, 5 marks are awarded: the candidate generally uses simple structures and vocabulary but on occasion attempts more complex language, e.g. an object pronoun (*je le promène*), irregular verb and reflexive verbs in the same sentence (*quand on se voit, on se dispute*), link words to lengthen sentences (*Ce serait bien parce que j'ai un copain qui habite à Bristol*). The three main time frames are referred to fairly successfully, and irregular verbs, reflexive verbs and the conditional are included.

Pronunciation is assumed to be generally good with a little intonation, making a mark of 3 suitable. A mark of 3 is also given for spontaneity and fluency as the performance is assumed to be a reasonably good standard, with some hesitation at times.

1. **Although the vocabulary used is mainly simple, there are examples of words that are less common. What do these words mean?**

   monoparental   *licence*   *gagner sa vie*   *parfait*

2. **Answer the following questions, giving as much detail as possible, using the words given above if relevant:**

   - Parle-moi de ta famille.

   - Tu aimerais aller à l'université?

   - Et comme métier plus tard?

Conversation 2: Themes 1 and 3

Passons à la conversation. Tu as choisi le thème numéro un. Parle-moi un peu de tes amis.

J'ai beaucoup de copains, garçons et filles, mais de vrais amis je n'en ai pas beaucoup. Mon meilleur ami s'appelle Cédric. Il a le même âge que moi et on se connait depuis longtemps. En fait, on était à l'école primaire ensemble.

Il est comment, Cédric?

Physiquement, il est plus grand que moi. Il a les yeux bleus et les cheveux bruns et courts. De personnalité, on se ressemble beaucoup. On a un peu les mêmes idées et on aime les mêmes choses.

Comme quoi, par exemple?

On est tous les deux sportifs. Lui, il adore faire de la natation. J'aime bien ça aussi mais moi, je préfère le foot. On fait toutes sortes d'activités ensemble. Le samedi par exemple, on va retrouver nos copains en ville et on passe l'après-midi à faire du shopping ou à nous promener. Avec les copains, c'est la compagnie qui compte.

Tu fais une grande différence entre les copains et les amis?

Oui, un copain est quelqu'un avec qui on sort ou on s'amuse. On se voit fréquemment et c'est agréable de passer de bons moments ensemble. Avec un ami, c'est un peu la même chose mais en plus, on peut parler de ses problèmes et se confier à lui. C'est quelqu'un sur qui on peut compter en cas de difficulté. Avez-vous un meilleur ami?

Oui, c'est important. Je suis d'accord avec toi. A ton avis, est-ce que la famille est plus importante dans la vie que les amis?

Je crois que oui. La famille sera toujours là pour nous aider avec nos petits problèmes. L'amitié c'est super mais ce n'est pas toujours aussi permanent que la famille. Par contre, il faut avouer qu'en ce qui concerne les problèmes personnels, il est plus facile d'en parler à un ami qu'à ses parents.

Est-ce que tu as l'intention d'avoir ta propre famille plus tard?
Oui, quand j'aurai vingt-cinq ans, j'aimerais bien me marier et avoir des enfants.

Tu ne veux pas vivre seul?
Absolument pas.

Pourquoi pas?
Je suis sûr que vivre seul doit être vraiment ennuyeux. Moi, j'aime beaucoup communiquer avec les autres.

Oui, mais tu peux communiquer par téléphone par exemple, non?
Je le sais mais ce n'est pas pareil.

Tu te sers beaucoup de ton portable?
Oui, énormément. Je m'en sers non seulement pour rester en contact avec mes amis mais aussi pour échanger des photos et des vidéos avec eux. Il m'est aussi utile pour faire de la recherche quand je fais mes devoirs.

C'est bien. Maintenant, passons au thème numéro 3. Parle-moi un peu de ton collège.
Je crois que c'est un bon collège. Il y a bien sûr certains aspects de la vie scolaire qui ne me plaisent pas mais, dans l'ensemble, je suis content d'y être.

Qu'est-ce qui ne te plaît pas?
Les sciences. Je les trouve ennuyeuses.

Quelle est ta matière préférée?
Le français. Je trouve ça facile et intéressant.

Et le règlement scolaire, qu'est-ce que tu en penses?
Il est utile mais je trouve que certaines règles ne sont pas nécessaires.

Donne-moi un exemple.
Il est interdit d'utiliser son portable.

Qu'est-ce qu'on devrait faire pour améliorer la situation au collège?
On devrait pouvoir choisir toutes les matières qu'on étudie. On devrait pas être obligé de porter un uniforme scolaire.

L'année prochaine, tu vas pouvoir choisir les matières que tu vas étudier, non?
Oui, j'ai l'intention d'aller au lycée et d'étudier le français, les maths et l'histoire.

Et après, tu voudrais aller à l'université?
Bien sûr. A l'avenir, j'espère devenir prof de français dans un lycée. Je pense que c'est une carrière fantastique. On travaille avec des jeunes qui ont choisi de continuer leurs études et aiment la matière qu'on enseigne. A mon avis, c'est un travail super.

Quels sont les inconvénients de cette profession, à ton avis?
Tout d'abord, il faut faire de longues études qui coûtent cher. Ensuite, il faut trouver un poste dans la région de notre choix. Ça, ça peut être difficile et prendre beaucoup de temps.

C'est vrai. Et si tu ne peux pas trouver un poste d'enseignant, que feras-tu?
Je chercherai un emploi dans la ville où habitent mes parents.

Je te souhaite bonne chance. Dis-moi, avant tout cela, il faut avoir de bons résultats d'examens cette année. Tu penses que ça va bien marcher?
Je l'espère. J'ai bien travaillé cette année et tous mes profs m'ont dit que je devrais avoir de bons résultats.

Excellent. Bon, c'est fini. Je te remercie.

Marks and commentary

	Communication	Range and accuracy of language	Pronunciation and intonation	Spontaneity and fluency	Total
Marks	10/10	10/10	5/5	5/5	**30/30**

This conversation is awarded the highest mark available. All the answers are developed and extended. Information is clearly communicated and opinions are given and explained convincingly. The two themes are covered in detail and both would last longer than the minimum 2 minute 30 seconds.

The conversation is given 10 marks for range and accuracy of language, as there are many complex linguistic structures and little repetition. A wide variety of complex structures and a wide range of vocabulary have been used. There are repetitions of words and phrases which could have been avoided (*je trouve*, *les mêmes*), but overall, the vocabulary is rich and varied. There are several examples of comparatives, *depuis*, all three time frames, negatives, the conditional, and emphatic pronouns.

The pronunciation and intonation are assumed to be excellent with good intonation, warranting a mark of 5. 5 marks are also given for spontaneity and fluency as the exchange is excellent with no obvious omissions or hesitations.

1. **Find seven different ways in which opinions are expressed.**

2. **Try and further develop the answers explaining:**

   - how communication face to face compares to communication by phone

   - what is boring about science

   - what is interesting about French

   - why it is frustrating not to be able to use your mobile phone in school.

Model answers and mark schemes

AQA GCSE French (9-1)

Higher Tier Paper 3 Reading

Time allowed: 1 hour

Instructions
- Answer **all** questions.
- Answer the questions in the spaces provided.
- In **Section A**, answer the questions in **English**. In **Section B**, answer the questions in **French**. In **Section C**, translate the passage into **English**.
- Cross through any work you do not want to be marked.

Information
- The marks for the questions are shown in brackets.
- The maximum mark for this paper is 60.
- You must **not** use a dictionary.

Please note: The Practice Paper questions and answers have not been written or approved by AQA.

Section A   Questions and answers in **English**

| 0 | 1 | **Obesity**

You read this French online article on obesity.

> L'obésité est devenue un problème qui affecte un nombre de personnes toujours grandissant. Que la cause en soit un problème médical, une mauvaise alimentation ou une combinaison de ces deux facteurs, il n'en reste pas moins que les conséquences peuvent être graves. Pour ceux qui en souffrent, il devient difficile de faire de l'exercice physique ou, dans les cas extrêmes, de se déplacer sans l'aide d'une personne ou d'un fauteuil roulant. De plus, le risque de crise cardiaque est plus élévé pour les personnes obèses. Si possible, il est impératif de perdre du poids. Il est aussi conseillé de se mettre sous surveillance médicale.

Which **four** statements are true? Write the correct letters in the boxes.

A	The number of people affected by obesity is stable.
B	Obesity is always the direct result of a poor diet.
C	Obesity has serious consequences.
D	It is impossible for obese people to get involved in physical activities.
E	People most seriously affected by obesity need help to move around.
F	Obese people are at a greater risk of a heart attack than most.
G	Losing weight is always possible.
H	It is advisable for obese people to be monitored by medical staff.

☐ ☐ ☐ ☐   **[4 marks]**

0 2 Holiday reviews

You read online holiday reviews on a French website.

Marcel
L'hôtel n'était pas mal, mais sans plus. Le seul problème, c'était qu'il était situé au bord d'une route où il y avait beaucoup de circulation. De plus, la ville en elle-même n'avait rien de spécial.

Manon
Il a fait un temps tellement mauvais que cela a gâché nos vacances. Pas possible d'aller à la plage ou de se baigner. Des magasins, ça, oui, on les a tous faits. J'en ai marre de faire du shopping.

Arthur
On avait loué un chalet dans les Alpes. Les vues sur les montagnes enneigées étaient extraordinaires. Dommage que le chauffage central ne marchait pas. Nos prochaines vacances, on les prendra en été.

Julie
Tout était parfait. On a fait des visites intéressantes. Le restaurant où on a pris nos repas était de première classe. Il faut toutefois avouer que le gîte manquait de confort et qu'il n'était pas propre quand on est arrivés.

> Sometimes, the answer to a question is not clearly stated in the text – you have to work it out from other clues. This applies to the first question here, where you have to look for clues about the time of year, rather than the person explicitly stating that they went on holiday in winter.

Write the name of the correct person in the box for each question.

0 2 . 1 Who had a winter holiday?

[1 mark]

0 2 . 2 Who had a terrible holiday?

[1 mark]

▶ Continued

0 2 . 3   Who was very happy with their holiday except

for the accommodation?

[1 mark]

0 2 . 4   Who found most aspects of their holiday

fairly average?

[1 mark]

0 3   **School rules**

You read the rules on a noticeboard at your Swiss partner school.

Les règles de vie scolaire
A   Il est essentiel d'arriver en cours à l'heure.
B   En cas d'absence, les élèves doivent, à leur retour, donner à leur professeur principal une lettre d'explication signée par leurs parents.
C   Il ne faut pas bavarder en classe.
D   Il est obligatoire de faire tous ses devoirs tous les jours.
E   Les élèves qui ne respectent pas le règlement recevront une retenue.
F   Les gros mots, le comportement violent, la drogue, les cigarettes et l'alcool sont interdits.
G   Les bijoux et le maquillage ne sont pas autorisés.
H   Il est indispensable de s'habiller de manière présentable.

Choose the rule which relates to each topic. Write the correct letter in the box.

0 3 . 1   Detentions   [1 mark]

0 3 . 2   Swearing   [1 mark]

0 3 . 3   Punctuality   [1 mark]

0 3 . 4   Chatting in lessons   [1 mark]

0 4   Being addicted to a mobile phone

Read this email Simon wrote to his friend Luc.

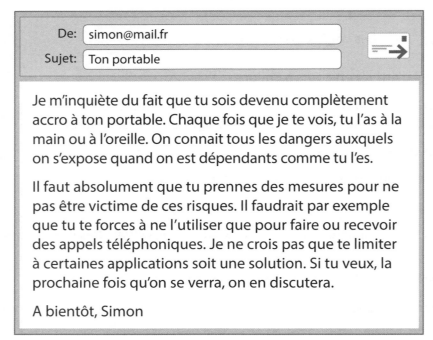

De: simon@mail.fr

Sujet: Ton portable

Je m'inquiète du fait que tu sois devenu complètement accro à ton portable. Chaque fois que je te vois, tu l'as à la main ou à l'oreille. On connait tous les dangers auxquels on s'expose quand on est dépendants comme tu l'es.

Il faut absolument que tu prennes des mesures pour ne pas être victime de ces risques. Il faudrait par exemple que tu te forces à ne l'utiliser que pour faire ou recevoir des appels téléphoniques. Je ne crois pas que te limiter à certaines applications soit une solution. Si tu veux, la prochaine fois qu'on se verra, on en discutera.

A bientôt, Simon

- Check that what you have written actually answers the question without ambiguity.
- Don't rely too much on cognates alone to work out the answers, e.g. 'limit – certain applications – solution' will not lead you to a clear answer to question 04.4.

Answer the questions in **English**.

0 4 . 1   What makes Simon think that his friend Luc is totally dependent on his phone?

_____

[1 mark]

0 4 . 2   Why is being dependent on a mobile phone a concern?

_____

[1 mark]

0 4 . 3   What solution to the problem does Simon suggest to Luc?

_____

[1 mark]

0 4 . 4   What other solution to the problem does Simon mention but then reject?

_____

[1 mark]

0	5

Volunteering

You read this call for volunteers from a Congolese charity.

Faites du bénévolat! Vous n'en tirerez que des satisfactions!

Notre association cherche à recruter des bénévoles qui pourraient offrir leurs services le lundi et le mardi entre huit heures et seize heures. Leurs tâches sont variées et sont susceptibles de changer d'une semaine à l'autre. L'important est d'être là pour ceux qui sont dans le besoin. Vous les aiderez en les conseillant ou en leur servant un repas chaud par exemple. Il y a de nombreuses manières de venir à leur secours.

Cette expérience sera inoubliable pour eux autant que pour vous. Vous aurez le plaisir de savoir, par exemple, que vous avez contribué à l'insertion dans notre société d'une famille étrangère qui ne parle pas français. Bien que votre générosité ne soit pas récompensée pécuniairement, soyez sans crainte, elle sera appréciée par tous, et cela vous apportera une profonde satisfaction.

Contactez-nous d'urgence, nous avons besoin de vous!

Which **four** statements are true? Write the correct letters in the boxes.

A	This charity is looking for someone who can work Monday to Friday.
B	When you volunteer, you don't know in advance what you will be doing.
C	You may be asked to cook a meal.
D	You will benefit greatly from the experience of helping others.
E	You won't be asked to deal with people who can't speak French.
F	You will not be paid for your work.
G	The work you do will be much appreciated by its recipients.
H	In case of emergency, you shouldn't hesitate to contact the organisation.

[4 marks]

| 0 6 | **A journey** |

Read this extract from the novel *'Un sac de billes'* by Joseph Joffo.

A présent, dit mon père, vous allez bien vous rappeler ce que je vais vous dire. Vous partez ce soir, vous prenez le métro jusqu'à la gare d'Austerlitz et là vous achèterez un billet pour Dax. Et là, il vous faudra passer la ligne*. Bien sûr, vous n'aurez pas de papiers pour passer, il faudra vous débrouiller. Tout près de Dax, vous irez dans un village qui s'appelle Hagetmau, là il y a des gens qui vous font passer la ligne. Une fois de l'autre côté, vous êtes sauvés. Vous êtes en France libre. Vos frères sont à Menton, je vous montrerai sur la carte tout à l'heure où ça se trouve, c'est tout près de la frontière italienne. Vous les retrouverez.

---

* la ligne = the border between 'occupied France' and 'free France'

- To answer the first question, look for a mode of transport. Don't be confused by the fact that there are two different words that suggest two different modes of transport. i.e. *le metro, la gare.*
- The information given to you about *la ligne* should not be ignored when answering the second question.
- Look for information in the last two sentences telling you what the two sons will be able to do in Menton.

Complete the sentences in **English**.

| 0 6 . 1 | Joseph and his brother will start the journey by

_____ .

[1 mark]

| 0 6 . 2 | In Hagetmau, they will need to find people who can

help them _____ .

[1 mark]

| 0 6 . 3 | They will then travel to Menton where they will be

able to _____ .

[1 mark]

0 7   **The importance of education**

You read this online report, published in France, on the importance of education.

> Dans la plupart des pays du monde, l'éducation des jeunes est obligatoire. Elle leur permet de développer leurs connaissances, de mieux comprendre ce qui se passe dans le monde et de vivre dans une société égalitaire. Cela concerne les garçons aussi bien que les filles. Il est à regretter toutefois que dans certains pays, les filles n'aient pas accès à cette éducation. Cette forme de sexisme n'est vraiment plus acceptable. De nos jours, chacun s'efforce de soutenir le mouvement pour l'égalité des sexes.

Write the correct letter in each box.

0 7 . 1   L'éducation des jeunes est obligatoire dans …

A	la majorité des pays.
B	quelques pays.
C	le monde entier.

[1 mark]

0 7 . 2   L'éducation développe …

A	les personnes qu'on connaît.
B	le sens de l'égalité.
C	notre compassion.

[1 mark]

0 7 . 3   Les pays qui refusent aux jeunes filles l'accès à l'éducation sont …

A	victimes de sexisme.
B	coupables de sexisme.
C	en faveur de l'égalité des sexes.

[1 mark]

| 0 | 8 | **Is marriage still popular?**

You read this online article on the topic of marriage.

Si vingt-cinq millions de Français sont aujourd'hui mariés, il n'en reste pas moins que la popularité du mariage est en déclin. L'année dernière, le nombre de personnes qui se sont mariées était moins de la moitié du nombre de celles qui l'ont fait en 1946. Il y a certes près de deux millions de personnes qui sont pacsées et trois millions qui vivent en concubinage. A quoi cela est-il dû? Peut-être au fait que la religion a moins d'impact maintenant qu'elle ne l'avait du temps de nos grands-parents. Peut-être aussi à la facilité avec laquelle les couples peuvent divorcer de nos jours.

> Two out of the three questions require an answer that involves numbers. Spot some numbers, e.g. *vingt-cinq millions*, and words linked with numbers, e.g. *la moitié*, but don't jump to conclusions and assume that they will be the answers required. You may have to add up numbers, for example, to get to the correct answer.

Answer the questions in **English**.

| 0 | 8 | . | 1 | What is significant about the fact that many more people got married in 1946, compared to last year?

_____

[1 mark]

| 0 | 8 | . | 2 | How many French people live in a couple but aren't married?

_____

[1 mark]

| 0 | 8 | . | 3 | Give one reason why there are fewer married couples these days than there were in the 1940s.

_____

[1 mark]

0 9   **Going to university**

Read this leaflet published by a French university.

> Si vous avez l'intention de faire des études supérieures, n'hésitez pas à nous contacter. Notre université a une réputation sans égale en ce qui concerne le taux d'étudiants qui trouvent un emploi à la fin de leurs études. Selon les sondages faits au fil des années, la qualité de l'enseignement que nos étudiants reçoivent est excellente et très appréciée. Question logement et nourriture, nos étudiants sont gâtés. Notre cité universitaire se compose de quatre cents chambres individuelles et le restaurant universitaire est ouvert à tous. Nous attendons votre demande avec plaisir.

Are these statements true (**T**), false (**F**) or not mentioned (**NM**)?

Write **T**, **F** or **NM** in each box.

0 9 . 1   This university is known for the high rate of employment among its graduates.

            [1 mark]

0 9 . 2   The quality of teaching is not as high as one might have expected.

            [1 mark]

0 9 . 3   University accommodation is offered to all students.

            [1 mark]

0 9 . 4   All students are welcome to use the university's canteen facilities.

            [1 mark]

Section B   Questions and answers in **French**

1 0   **Les bienfaits de partir en vacances**

Lisez ce que pensent ces touristes français des vacances.

Jade
Pour moi, c'est la meilleure période de l'année car c'est l'occasion de ne pas faire grand-chose et de me reposer.

Mohamed
Comme je travaille six jours par semaine, à part le dimanche, je ne vois pas le reste de ma famille ou mes amis très souvent.

Elodie
Une fois par an, c'est bien de se dépayser un peu, de changer d'environnement, de prendre l'air frais de la mer par exemple.

Simon
C'est le seul moment de l'année où on peut faire ce qu'on veut toute la journée. On n'est pas obligés de faire quoi que ce soit.

Stéphanie
A condition qu'il fasse beau, on peut aller à la plage et se faire bronzer.

> - Look out for synonyms or paraphrases, e.g. relaxing = not doing much = resting.
> - Take care: both Elodie and Stéphanie mention the seaside but only one statement refers to an activity on the beach.

C'est quelle personne? Ecrivez le bon prénom dans les cases.

1 0 . 1   C'est l'occasion de passer un peu plus de temps que d'habitude avec mes copains.

[1 mark]

1 0 . 2   On est libres de faire n'importe quelle activité à toute heure de la journée.

[1 mark]

▶ **Continued**

1 0 . 3 C'est bien de passer une semaine ou deux ailleurs.

[1 mark]

1 0 . 4 J'adore ça mais il faut faire attention à ne pas prendre de coups de soleil.

[1 mark]

1 0 . 5 Comme on n'est pas au travail, on en profite pour se relaxer.

[1 mark]

| 1 | 1 | **Ma petite amie**

Lisez le message d'Arnaud à son ami Marcel.

> J'ai rencontré Camille le mois dernier en ville. Elle était avec ses copines et moi avec mes copains. On est tous allés à la plage et j'ai commencé à parler à Camille qui est super sympa. On a trouvé qu'on avait beaucoup de points en commun, comme aller au cinéma par exemple, et en plus on a bien rigolé. On a décidé de sortir ensemble et depuis, je la vois presque tous les jours. On s'entend particulièrement bien et jusqu'à maintenant, on ne s'est jamais disputés. Je suis super content qu'elle soit ma petite amie et j'espère que cela va durer. Elle a le même âge que moi et je crois que je l'aime.

Complétez les phrases. Ecrivez la bonne lettre dans chaque case.

| 1 | 1 | . | 1 | La première fois qu'Arnaud et Camille se sont rencontrés, ils étaient …

A	à la plage.
B	en ville.
C	seuls.

[1 mark]

| 1 | 1 | . | 2 | Camille …

A	a des goûts différents de ceux d'Arnaud.
B	et Arnaud ont le même sens de l'humour.
C	n'aime pas aller voir un film.

[1 mark]

| 1 | 1 | . | 3 | Arnaud et Camille …

A	s'entendent à merveille.
B	se disputent rarement.
C	se voient une fois par semaine.

[1 mark]

| 1 | 1 | . | 4 | Camille …

A	est amoureuse d'Arnaud.
B	est un peu plus âgée qu'Arnaud.
C	a un petit ami qui l'adore.

[1 mark]

| 1 | 2 |

Deux métiers importants

Le grand-frère de votre correspondant(e) cherche un travail et vous montre ces brochures spécialisées dans le recrutement des jeunes.

Pompier/Pompière

Votre rôle principal est évidemment d'éteindre le feu lorsqu'un incendie se déclare. En faisant cela, vous aurez souvent l'occasion de sauver quelqu'un dont la vie est en danger. Cet aspect de votre travail est celui qui vous apportera le plus de satisfaction. Vous devez bien sûr être disponible à toute heure en cas d'urgence.

Infirmier/Infirmière

Que vous soyez infirmier/infirmière à domicile ou que vous travailliez dans un hôpital, l'impact que vous avez sur la santé physique des malades est, bien entendu, important. Toutefois, ce qui touche le plus les malades est la manière dont ils sont traités. Ils apprécient votre gentillesse et cette reconnaissance est ce qui rend le travail très gratifiant. Vous serez de temps en temps de service le weekend, il faut le dire, mais cela en vaut la peine.

Pour chaque profession, mentionnez **un** avantage et **un** inconvénient. Complétez les cases en **français**.

| 1 | 2 |.| 1 | Pompier/Pompière

Avantage	Inconvénient

[2 marks]

| 1 | 2 |.| 2 | Infirmier/Infirmière

Avantage	Inconvénient

[2 marks]

1 3 Les incendies de forêt

Lisez cet article français en ligne.

Il est navrant de constater que, d'année en année, les feux de forêt sont devenus de plus en plus fréquents, particulièrement en juillet et en août. C'est en effet la période de l'année où il pleut le moins en général. On peut essayer d'attribuer cette fréquence des incendies aux changements climatiques, au réchauffement de la terre ou à la sécheresse. Dans bien des cas lorsqu'un incendie se déclare, c'est en effet une cause naturelle qui en est à l'origine. Il est toutefois indéniable que beaucoup sont la conséquence de l'activité humaine, qu'elle soit d'ordre criminel ou accidentel.

Comment pouvons-nous protéger notre environnement et empêcher de telles catastrophes? L'éducation a sans aucun doute son rôle à jouer. Les collèges pourraient par exemple enseigner aux élèves l'importance des forêts d'un point de vue environnemental. On devrait aussi faire passer des lois interdisant au public d'allumer des feux et de fumer en forêt. Il faut absolument agir rapidement pour résoudre le problème des incendies de forêt.

- Look for synonyms e.g. *souvent* = *fréquents*, *en été* = *en juillet et en août*.
- To ascertain whether the statement is true or false, make sure you consider every word of it e.g. in question 13.2 *presque tous*… Your understanding of these two words will guide you to the correct answer.

Décidez si les phrases sont vraies (**V**), fausses (**F**) ou pas mentionnées (**PM**).

Ecrivez **V**, **F** ou **PM**.

1 3 . 1 Il y a souvent des feux de forêt en été.

[1 mark]

1 3 . 2 Les causes naturelles sont à l'origine de presque tous les feux de forêt.

[1 mark]

1 3 . 3 Si on déclenche un incendie criminel, on risque une longue peine de prison.

[1 mark]

▶ Continued

1 3 . 4 L'éducation joue un rôle important dans la prévention des incendies.

[1 mark]

1 3 . 5 Faire des feux en forêt ne devrait pas être permis.

[1 mark]

Section C   Translation into **English**

| 1 | 4 |

Your friend has seen this post on social media and asks you to translate it for him into **English**.

> En fumant des cigarettes, certains jeunes aiment donner l'impression qu'ils sont adultes. Ce produit est très dangereux car il est facile d'en devenir dépendant. Une fois l'habitude prise, il est difficile de s'arrêter. Le problème est que le tabac est la cause principale du cancer du poumon, une maladie qui tue.

[9 marks]

_____

_____

_____

_____

_____

_____

_____

_____

END OF QUESTIONS

Answers and mark schemes

AQA GCSE French Higher Practice Papers © Oxford University Press 2020. Photocopying prohibited.

AQA GCSE French (9-1)

PRACTICE PAPER

Higher Tier Paper 4 Writing

Time allowed: 1 hour 15 minutes

Instructions

- You must answer **three** questions.
- You must answer **either** Question 1.1 **or** Question 1.2. Do not answer both of these questions.
- You must answer **either** Question 2.1 **or** Question 2.2. Do not answer both of these questions.
- You must answer Question 3.
- Answer all questions in **French**.
- Answer the questions in the spaces provided.
- Cross through any work you do not want to be marked.

Information

- The marks for the questions are shown in brackets.
- The maximum mark for this paper is 60.
- You must **not** use a dictionary during this test.
- In order to score the highest marks for Question 1.1/Question 1.2, you must write something about each bullet point. You must use a variety of vocabulary and structures and include your opinions.
- In order to score the highest marks for Question 2.1/Question 2.2, you must write something about both bullet points. You must use a variety of vocabulary and structures and include your opinions and reasons.

Please note: The Practice Paper questions and answers have not been written or approved by AQA.

Answer **either** Question 1.1 **or** Question 1.2.
You must **not** answer **both** of these questions.

___

EITHER Question 1.1

| 0 | 1 | . | 1 | Vous écrivez un article sur le weekend
pour un magazine français.

Décrivez:

- ce que vous faites d'habitude le weekend

- vos activités le weekend dernier

- ce que vous allez faire le weekend prochain

- ce que vous pensez du weekend en général.

Ecrivez environ **90** mots en **français**. Répondez à chaque aspect de la question.

[16 marks]

> - You must make an effort to cover all the bullet points. Not covering one can reduce the marks available for content from 10 to 6.
> - Identify the bullet points which require opinions and different tenses.

OR Question 1.2

| 0 | 1 | . | 2 | Vous décrivez votre meilleur(e) ami(e)
pour votre blog.

Décrivez:

- son apparence physique

- son caractère

- ce que vous avez fait ensemble le weekend dernier

- ce que vous ferez ensemble pendant les grandes vacances.

Ecrivez environ **90** mots en **français**. Répondez à chaque aspect de la question.

[16 marks]

> - First work out what the bullet points mean. In this question, there are quite a few cognates, which should help you.
> - The third bullet point requires you to write about a past activity. If you haven't done anything to mention here, you can invent something; remember to write about it in the perfect tense.
> - Make sure you use a future time frame when addressing the last bullet point.

Answer **either** Question 2.1 **or** Question 2.2.
You must **not** answer **both** of these questions.

EITHER Question 2.1

| 0 | 2 |.| 1 | Vous décrivez votre avenir et vos aspirations pour votre blog.

Décrivez:

- ce que vous avez l'intention de faire l'année prochaine.

- ce que vous aimeriez faire une fois votre scolarité terminée.

> - There is no need for equal coverage of the bullet points, but make sure you provide sufficient information for both points and that your response overall is around 150 words.
> - Plan your response carefully: for example, for the second bullet you could make a list of relevant sub-topics to include.
> - Pay attention to verb tenses and time phrases in the bullet points: they will guide you to use the correct tense in your response.
> - Try to vary your vocabulary by using synonyms rather than repeating words.

Ecrivez environ **150** mots en **français**. Répondez aux deux aspects de la question.

[32 marks]

OR Question 2.2

| 0 | 2 |.| 2 | Vous écrivez un article sur les vacances pour le magazine de votre collège partenaire français.

Décrivez:

- ce que vous avez fait l'été dernier

- ce que vous espérez faire à Noël.

> - Plan your response by making a list of what you did during last year's summer holiday, i.e. activities you did or places you visited, and what you hope to do at Christmas.
> - Include as much detail as possible by using linking words and complex structures such as irregular verbs, negatives, comparatives, reflexive verbs, and verbs in different tenses.
> - When finished, check your work for accuracy. Check also that you have used a variety of vocabulary.

Ecrivez environ **150** mots en **français**. Répondez aux deux aspects de la question.

[32 marks]

0 3   Translate the following passage into **French**.

> I had a job interview yesterday. It was not easy to answer some of the questions.
> I was lucky because I was offered the job! Next Monday, I will be an electrician.
> At last, I am going to earn some money – ten euros an hour. I don't like asking
> my parents for money.

[12 marks]

- There are marks available for conveying key messages, so if you don't
  know a word, try to find a similar word rather than leaving it out of the
  translation altogether.
- Both the perfect tense and future tense are required in this task, so make
  sure that you use the correct auxiliary verb and that your endings are
  correct.

_____

_____

_____

_____

_____

_____

_____

_____

_____

_____

END OF QUESTIONS

Model answers and mark schemes

AQA GCSE French (9-1)

Higher Tier Paper 1 Listening

Time allowed: 45 minutes
(including 5 minutes' reading time before the test)

You will need no other materials.
The pauses are pre-recorded for this test.

Information
- The marks for the questions are shown in brackets. The maximum mark for this paper is 50.
- You must **not** use a dictionary.

Advice
This is what you should do for each item.
- After the question number is announced, there will be a pause to allow you to read the instructions and questions.
- Listen carefully to the recording and read the questions again.
- Listen to the recording again, and then answer the questions.
- When the next question is about to start you will hear a bleep.
- You may write at any time during the test.
- In **Section A**, answer the questions in **English**. In **Section B**, answer the questions in **French**.
- You must answer all the questions in the spaces provided. Do not write on blank pages.
- Write neatly and put down all the information you are asked to give.
- **You must not ask questions or interrupt during the test.**
- You have five minutes to read through the question paper. You may make notes during this time. You may turn to the questions now.
- **The test starts now.**

Listen to the audio

Please note: The Practice Paper questions and answers have not been written or approved by AQA.

Section A   Questions and answers in **English**

Working as a team

Listen to four French people taking part in a survey on teamwork.

What do they think about teamwork?

For a negative opinion, write **N**.

For a positive opinion, write **P**.

For a positive and negative opinion, write **P+N**.

| 0 | 1 | | [1 mark] |

| 0 | 2 | | [1 mark] |

| 0 | 3 | | [1 mark] |

| 0 | 4 | | [1 mark] |

| 0 | 5 | **What shall we do this weekend?**

You are spending the day with your French exchange partner, Julie, at her school. You ask her what will happen at the weekend.

Listen to the conversation. Choose **three** sentences that are **true** and write the correct letters in the boxes.

A	Today, after lunch, Julie and her friends will go shopping in town.
B	Julie would like to talk to her friends about the coming weekend.
C	Before lunch, Julie will meet her friends in the playground.
D	Julie likes meeting other friends in town at the weekend.
E	On Sundays, Julie often stays at a friend's house.
F	Julie spends Sundays with her family.

[3 marks]

My house

Kevin will soon be hosting his French partner Alain, on a school exchange. In a phone call, Alain asks Kevin about his house.

Listen and choose the correct answer to complete each sentence.

Write the correct letter in each box.

Answer both parts of question 6.

`0 6 . 1` It takes five minutes to go from Kevin's house to the town centre …

A	on foot.
B	by bus.
C	by bike.

[1 mark]

`0 6 . 2` Kevin goes to school …

A	by car.
B	using the school bus.
C	on foot.

[1 mark]

Answer both parts of question 7.

`0 7 . 1` Alain will have …

A	to share a room.
B	his own room.
C	an en-suite bathroom.

[1 mark]

`0 7 . 2` In the garage, there is Kevin's …

A	mother's car.
B	father's car.
C	father's bike.

[1 mark]

Protecting the environment

You are at your French partner's school. The teacher asks what students do to protect the environment.

For each speaker, choose the correct action from the list and write the correct letter in the box.

A	Recycling
B	Showering rather than taking baths
C	Using public transport
D	Cleaning the beach
E	Saving gas and electricity
F	Taking the school bus or walking
G	Belonging to a club for the protection of the environment
H	Refusing to use plastic bags
I	Never throwing rubbish on the ground
J	Protecting animal life by being vegan

0 8 ☐ **[1 mark]**

0 9 ☐ **[1 mark]**

1 0 ☐ **[1 mark]**

1 1 ☐ **[1 mark]**

Career choices

You listen to people talking about their jobs on French radio.

For each person, choose **two** statements that are **true** and write the correct letters in the boxes.

1 2		
	A	It is quite difficult to find a job as a dentist.
	B	A dentist usually does not work long hours.
	C	Dentists are well paid.
	D	A dentist needs an assistant to help him/her.

☐ ☐ **[2 marks]**

1 3		
	A	Teaching is not a well-paid job.
	B	This teacher likes the long summer holidays.
	C	Young children are not always easy company.
	D	Teaching is a rewarding job.

☐ ☐ **[2 marks]**

1 4		
	A	Postmen start their working day early.
	B	Postmen finish their working day in the late afternoon.
	C	On wet days, postmen start work later in the morning.
	D	This postman is happy with the money he earns.

☐ ☐ **[2 marks]**

Attitudes towards sport

While on a trip to France, you hear four students talking about their attitudes to sport. Complete the sentences in **English**.

| 1 | 5 |

Rugby is a sport that Lucie likes to _____.

[1 mark]

| 1 | 6 |

To keep fit, Arthur _____ three times a week.

[1 mark]

| 1 | 7 |

Marie _____ to exercise.

[1 mark]

| 1 | 8 |

When he is not at home, Richard likes _____.

[1 mark]

Town vs countryside

You listen to this podcast in which a teenager compares living in town with living in the countryside.

Complete the boxes in **English**.

| 1 | 9 |

What was **one** advantage and **one** disadvantage of living in town?

Advantage	Disadvantage

[2 marks]

| 2 | 0 |

What is **one** advantage and **one** disadvantage of living in the country?

Advantage	Disadvantage

[2 marks]

Further education advice

At your French partner's school, the careers adviser is addressing students who are soon to leave school.

Listen to his advice and complete the sentences in **English**.

Answer all parts of the question.

2 1 . 1 The careers adviser recommends that students think about future plans _____.

[1 mark]

2 1 . 2 Students should consider whether their dream job requires _____.

[1 mark]

2 1 . 3 If a student does not gain good grades in exams, the adviser recommends _____.

[1 mark]

2 1 . 4 For students who do not wish to further their studies, he advises _____.

[1 mark]

2 1 . 5 Finally, he _____ to all the students.

[1 mark]

Young children and mobile phones

While on holiday in France, you listen to a radio phone-in programme about young children and mobile phones.

Answer the questions in **English**.

| 2 | 2 | What should three-year-olds focus on, according to this caller?

_____

[1 mark]

| 2 | 3 | What risk does this speaker see in primary school children having a mobile phone?

_____

[1 mark]

| 2 | 4 | Why is the caller in favour of small children having mobile phones?

_____

[1 mark]

| 2 | 5 | Whose responsibility is it, according to this caller, to introduce children to technology?

_____

[1 mark]

| 2 | 6 | When should children carry a mobile phone, according to this speaker?

_____

[1 mark]

| 2 | 7 | Why does this speaker think it is not necessary for children to have mobile phones?

_____

[1 mark]

Section B   Questions and answers in **French**

Témoignage d'un SDF

Vous entendez ce témoignage d'un SDF à la radio belge.

Répondez aux trois aspects de la question 28 en **français**.

`2 8 . 1`   Qu'est-il arrivé à ce SDF cet après-midi?

_____

[1 mark]

`2 8 . 2`   Pourquoi est-il inquiet à l'idée de dormir dehors?

_____

[1 mark]

`2 8 . 3`   Que va-t-il faire pour essayer de trouver du travail?

_____

[1 mark]

La télé, ça vous plaît?

Votre ami français parle de la télé avec ses amis. Qu'est-ce qu'ils pensent de la télé?

Pour une opinion négative, écrivez **N**.

Pour une opinion positive, écrivez **P**.

Pour une opinion positive et négative, écrivez **P+N**.

`2 9`   ⬚   [1 mark]

`3 0`   ⬚   [1 mark]

`3 1`   ⬚   [1 mark]

`3 2`   ⬚   [1 mark]

La pause-déjeuner

Vous êtes au collège en France avec votre partenaire d'échange. Vous parlez de la pause-déjeuner avec vos nouveaux amis français.

Complétez les phrases. Ecrivez la bonne lettre dans la case.

3 3   Lucy …

A	fait ses devoirs.
B	rentre chez elle.
C	mange à la cantine.

[1 mark]

3 4   Michel …

A	aime parler à ses copains.
B	fait des jeux sur son portable.
C	joue au foot avec ses copains quand il pleut.

[1 mark]

3 5   Mélanie …

A	rentre chez elle.
B	contacte ses amies avec son portable.
C	va à un club de technologie.

[1 mark]

END OF QUESTIONS

Answers and mark schemes

AQA GCSE French Higher Practice Papers © Oxford University Press 2020. Photocopying prohibited.

AQA GCSE French (9-1)

PRACTICE PAPER

Higher Tier Paper 2 Speaking

Time allowed: 10–12 minutes
(+12 minutes' supervised preparation time)

Candidate's material – Role-play and Photo card

Instructions
- During the preparation time you must prepare the Role-play card and Photo card given to you.
- You may make notes during the preparation time on the paper provided by your teacher-examiner. Do not write on the stimulus cards.
- Hand your notes and both stimulus cards to the teacher-examiner before the General Conversation.
- You must ask the teacher-examiner at least one question in the General Conversation.

Information
- The test will last a maximum of 12 minutes and will consist of a Role-play (approximately 2 minutes) and a Photo card (approximately 3 minutes), followed by a General Conversation (between 5 and 7 minutes) based on your nominated Theme and the remaining Theme which has not been covered in the Photo card.
- You must **not** use a dictionary at any time during the test. This includes the preparation time.

Teacher's scripts

Please note: The Practice Paper questions and answers have not been written or approved by AQA.

ROLE-PLAY 1

CANDIDATE'S ROLE

Instructions to candidates

Your teacher will play the part of your French friend and will speak first.

You should address your friend as *tu*.

When you see this – **!** – you will have to respond to something you have not prepared.

When you see this – **?** – you will have to ask a question.

Tu parles à ton ami(e) suisse du dernier repas que tu as pris au restaurant.

- Repas. Où et avec qui.

- Ce que tu as mangé et bu.

- Repas – opinion (**deux** détails).

- **!**

- **?** Activités le weekend prochain.

ROLE-PLAY 2

CANDIDATE'S ROLE

Instructions to candidates

Your teacher will play the part of the mother/father of your French friend and will speak first.

You should address your friend's parent as *vous*.

When you see this – **!** – you will have to respond to something you have not prepared.

When you see this – **?** – you will have to ask a question.

> Vous êtes en France en échange scolaire. Vous parlez de vos vacances à la mère/au père de votre correspondant(e).
>
> - Destination de vacances préférée.
>
> - Activités (**deux** détails).
>
> - Choix d'hébergement et raison.
>
> - **!**
>
> - **?** Activités en ville.

ROLE-PLAY 3

CANDIDATE'S ROLE

Instructions to candidates

Your teacher will play the part of your friend and will speak first.

You should address your friend as *tu*.

When you see this – **!** – you will have to respond to something you have not prepared.

When you see this – **?** – you will have to ask a question.

Tu parles de ton futur métier avec ton ami(e) suisse.

- Futur métier – **deux** possibilités.

- Premier choix. Raison.

- **Un** avantage de ce métier.

- **!**

- **?** Futur métier.

Card A   **Candidate's Photo card**

- Look at the photo during the preparation period.

- Make any notes you wish to on an additional piece of paper.

- Your teacher will ask you questions about the photo and about topics related to **free-time activities**.

Your teacher will ask you the following three questions and then **two more questions** which you have not prepared.

- Qu'est-ce qu'il y a sur la photo?

- Qu'est-ce qu'il y a pour ceux qui aiment le sport dans ta ville?

- Est-ce que tu as déjà fait du skateboard ou du patin à roulettes?

Card B   **Candidate's Photo card**

- Look at the photo during the preparation period.

- Make any notes you wish to on an additional piece of paper.

- Your teacher will ask you questions about the photo and about topics related to **global issues**.

Your teacher will ask you the following three questions and then **two more questions** which you have not prepared.

- Qu'est-ce qu'il y a sur la photo?

- Quel est le problème environnemental le plus grave dans ton pays?

- Qu'est-ce que tu as fait récemment pour la protection de l'environnement?

Card C   **Candidate's Photo card**

- Look at the photo during the preparation period.

- Make any notes you wish to on an additional piece of paper.

- Your teacher will ask you questions about the photo and about topics related to **my studies** and **life at school/college**.

Your teacher will ask you the following three questions and then **two more questions** which you have not prepared.

- Qu'est-ce qu'il y a sur la photo?

- Comment était ton école primaire?

- Tu préfères ton collège ou ton école primaire? Pourquoi?

GENERAL CONVERSATION

The Photo card is followed by a General Conversation. The first part of the conversation will be on a theme nominated by the candidate and the second part on the other theme not covered by the Photo card. The total time for the General Conversation will be between 5 and 7 minutes and a similar amount of time should be spent on each theme. Here is a reminder of the three themes:

- Identity and culture

- Local, national, international and global areas of interest

- Current and future study and employment

The following pages show two examples of the general conversation with accompanying commentary on how these conversations would be marked, followed by tasks.

Conversation 1: Themes 2 and 3

Passons à la conversation. Tu as choisi le thème numéro deux. Parle-moi un peu de ta ville.
J'habite à Brighton. C'est une grande ville située dans le sud du pays, au bord de la mer.

C'est bien comme ville?
Oui, c'est très animé.

Qu'est-ce qu'on peut y faire?
Tous les sports nautiques. On peut aussi faire du shopping. Il y a beaucoup de magasins.

Et toi, qu'est-ce que tu aimes faire en ville?
J'aime bien faire les magasins avec mes copains.

Qu'est-ce que tu n'aimes pas à Brighton?
La circulation.

C'est un problème?
Oui, il y a trop de voitures.

Qu'est-ce qu'on peut faire pour résoudre ce problème?
Utiliser les transports en commun.

Tu prends souvent le bus?
Non. En général, je me déplace à pied ou à vélo.

Il y a d'autres problèmes à Brighton?
Oui, bien sûr. L'air est pollué.

C'est dû à quoi?
Au nombre de voitures et aussi à l'industrie.

Il y a des solutions à ces problèmes?
Je pense qu'il faut encourager les gens à utiliser les transports en commun.

Et en ce qui concerne l'industrie?
Il faut avoir un quartier industriel en dehors de la ville.

Parlons d'autre chose. Raconte-moi tes dernières vacances.
Je suis allé en France avec ma famille.

Pour combien de temps?
Une semaine.

Il a fait beau?
Oui, tous les jours.

Vous y êtes allés en avion?
Non, on a pris notre voiture puis le ferry de Newhaven à Dieppe.

Vous avez logé dans un hôtel?
Non, on a fait du camping.

Qu'est-ce que vous avez fait d'intéressant en France?
On a visité Paris. J'ai vu l'Arc de Triomphe et je suis monté en haut de la tour Eiffel.

Super. Qu'est-ce que tu as pensé de tes vacances?
J'ai beaucoup aimé mes vacances.

Tu as de la chance. Maintenant passons au thème numéro 3. Parle-moi de ton école.
Je n'aime pas beaucoup mon collège. Il est trop grand. Il y a plus de mille élèves.

Décris une journée scolaire typique.
Je vais au collège en voiture avec ma mère le matin. J'arrive vers huit heures et demie. Je parle avec mes copains et à neuf heures, le premier cours commence. On a trois cours le matin et deux l'après-midi. A la pause-déjeuner, je vais à la cantine. On finit à quinze heures.

Qu'est-ce que tu fais à la récréation?
Je vais dans la cour où je retrouve mes copains. J'aime bien parler avec eux.

Tu t'entends bien avec tes profs?
Oui, sauf avec le prof d'histoire. Il est trop sévère.

Quelle est ta matière préférée?
L'anglais.

Tu vas continuer tes études d'anglais l'année prochaine?
Oui, j'irai au lycée. Je voudrais étudier l'anglais, la musique et l'art dramatique.

Pas le français?
Non. Je trouve le français assez difficile.

Oui, je comprends. Quel travail aimerais-tu faire plus tard dans la vie?
Je ne suis pas sûr. Peut-être un travail dans le domaine artistique.

Je vois. Que font tes parents comme travail?
Mon père est mécanicien et ma mère est institutrice.

Ils aiment leur travail?
Oui, surtout ma mère. Elle adore les enfants. Et vous, vous aimez votre travail?

Oui, beaucoup. Tu aimerais être prof comme moi?
Non, je ne voudrais pas travailler dans une école toute ma vie.

Je comprends. Merci bien. Nous avons fini.

Marks and commentary

	Communication	Range and accuracy of language	Pronunciation and intonation	Spontaneity and fluency	Total
Marks	4/10	4/10	3/5	3/5	**14/30**

This conversation is given 4 marks for communication as the responses are quite short, with extended answers occasionally provided, e.g. description of a typical school day. Clear information is given, along with six different opinions and an explanation on one occasion. For a slightly higher mark to be awarded, it is necessary to develop answers more frequently and to explain opinions more often. A question is correctly asked (about whether the teacher-examiner likes his/her job).

The conversation is awarded 4 marks for range and accuracy of language as reference is made to past events in sentences that contain a verb, and also to future events, either by using the future tense *or je voudrais* plus a verb. Irregular verbs are used correctly. Overall, though, the language and vocabulary displayed are kept very simple. Questions are occasionally answered in a few words without a verb. Most sentences are short and apart from two uses of *et*, there is no use of any other link words such as *mais*, *car*, *parce que* that would allow longer sentences.

Pronunciation is assumed to be reasonable with a little intonation, making a mark of 3 suitable.

3 marks are given for spontaneity and fluency as the performance is assumed to be of a reasonably good standard with some hesitations but the delivery has a reasonable pace.

> 1. **Find examples of:**
>   - the perfect tense
>   - the perfect tense with *avoir* and with *être* in the same sentence.
>   - words related to school and the school day

> **2.** **Answer the following questions for yourself, developing the answers as fully as possible. Include complex structures and as wide a range of vocabulary as you can.**
>
> - Raconte-moi tes dernières vacances. Qu'est-ce que tu as pensé de tes vacances?
>
> - Décris une journée scolaire typique.

Conversation 2: Themes 2 and 3

Passons à la conversation. Tu as choisi le thème numéro deux. Parle-moi de tes activités pendant les vacances scolaires.
D'habitude, je pars en vacances avec ma famille pour une quinzaine de jours. En général, on va au pays de Galles, au bord de la mer. Ça me plaît beaucoup parce que c'est vraiment différent de là où on habite.

Tu habites où exactement?
A Slough, au centre-ville.

Comment trouves-tu Slough?
C'est une grande ville un peu comme toutes les grandes villes. On peut faire toutes sortes d'activités. Moi, j'aime bien sortir en ville avec mes copines et faire les magasins. C'est aussi super pour les activités sportives.

Est-ce qu'il y a des problèmes à Slough?
Bien sûr. On a des problèmes environnementaux comme la pollution de l'air par exemple. Le chômage et la pauvreté sont aussi évidents en ville.

Oui, je vois. L'année dernière, tu es restée à Slough ou est-ce que tu es partie en vacances?
Nous sommes allés à Rhyl, au nord du pays de Galles. Mes parents avaient loué une petite maison pour deux semaines. Il n'a pas plu une seule fois. On s'est bien amusés.

Et l'année prochaine, tu aimerais y retourner?
Peut-être. Ce qui me plairait le plus, ce serait de visiter la France. Je n'y suis jamais allée.

Tu as visité d'autres pays?
Oui, j'ai fait un échange scolaire. J'ai passé une semaine à Barcelone, une ville que j'ai trouvée fantastique. Est-ce que vous avez déjà visité l'Espagne?

Oui, plusieurs fois. Qu'est-ce qui t'a plu en particulier?
La ville, les sorties et les fêtes qu'on a faites. L'année prochaine, ce sera bien parce que ma copine viendra passer une semaine chez moi. Elle est super sympa.

Qu'est-ce que vous ferez quand elle viendra?
Pour le moment, je ne sais pas mais j'aimerais lui montrer ce que je trouve intéressant ici.

C'est-à-dire quoi?
Windsor et son château par exemple. Je suis certaine qu'une journée à Londres lui plairait bien. Je n'ai pas encore décidé. On verra.

Maintenant passons au thème numéro 3. Ton collège, il est bien?
Oui, je crois que c'est le meilleur collège du coin. Les résultats d'examens le prouvent.

Tu travailles bien?
Je pense que oui et j'espère avoir de bonnes notes à tous les examens que je vais passer.

Quelle est ta matière préférée?
Le français, sans aucun doute. A mon avis, il est important d'apprendre une langue étrangère.

Pourquoi cela?
Parce que tout le monde ne parle pas anglais. Quand on visite un autre pays, on devrait faire l'effort de parler au moins quelques mots de leur langue.

Il y a des matières que tu n'aimes pas?
Je trouve que les maths sont vraiment difficiles. De plus, le prof n'est pas très sympa.

Quels sont tes projets pour l'année prochaine?
Mes parents pensent que je devrais aller au lycée et je suis tout à fait d'accord avec eux. J'aimerais bien étudier le français, l'anglais et l'espagnol.

Tu as l'intention d'aller à l'université?
Si mes résultats sont bons, ça me plairait de faire une licence de français. Plus tard, j'ai l'intention d'enseigner le français dans un collège.

Pourquoi as-tu choisi ce métier?
Parce que j'aime beaucoup la compagnie des jeunes et aussi parce que l'éducation est une chose très importante dans la vie.

Et si par hasard tu échoues dans tes études?
Dans ce cas, je travaillerai dans l'entreprise de mon père.

Qu'est-ce qu'il a comme entreprise?
Il est comptable et il travaille à son compte. Il a deux employés qui l'aident.

Parfait. Je te souhaite bonne chance pour l'avenir.
Merci.

Marks and commentary

	Communication	Range and accuracy of language	Pronunciation and intonation	Spontaneity and fluency	Total
Marks	9/10	10/10	5/5	5/5	**29/30**

This conversation is given 9 marks for communication as answers are developed in a way that is always entirely clear. Lots of opinions are offered which are almost always justified. A question is asked of the teacher-examiner at an appropriate point. The two themes are covered in detail and both last longer than the minimum 2 minute 30 seconds, so there is no penalty (–2) for a short theme.

There are 10 marks for range and accuracy of language as there are complex linguistic structures and little repetition. A range of different tenses and irregular verbs are used successfully. Object pronouns (*le, l', lui, y*) are used, as well as linking words to extend answers (*mais, parce que*). There are several different ways of expressing an opinion in the conversation and a good range of vocabulary: *le chômage, la pauvreté, échange scolaire, prouver, passer un examen, une langue étrangère, être d'accord, une licence, enseigner, une entreprise, comptable, à son compte.* The only aspect of this conversation that could have been improved is the occasional short answers.

The pronunciation and intonation are assumed to be consistently good, warranting a mark of 5. The conversation is also given 5 marks for spontaneity and fluency as the exchange is of an excellent standard and proceeds at a good pace.

> **Answer the teacher-examiner's questions yourself.**
>
> - Develop all your answers.
>
> - Include your opinions and explain them.
>
> - Include complex structures and as wide a range of vocabulary as you can.

Model answers and mark schemes

Higher Tier Paper 3 Reading

Time allowed: 1 hour

Instructions
- Answer **all** questions.
- Answer the questions in the spaces provided.
- In **Section A**, answer the questions in **English**. In **Section B**, answer the questions in **French**. In **Section C**, translate the passage into **English**.
- Cross through any work you do not want to be marked.

Information
- The marks for the questions are shown in brackets.
- The maximum mark for this paper is 60.
- You must **not** use a dictionary.

Please note: The Practice Paper questions and answers have not been written or approved by AQA.

Section A   Questions and answers in **English**

| 0 | 1 | **Our twin town**

Arthur is on an exchange visit to the UK. You read one of the messages he sends to his parents.

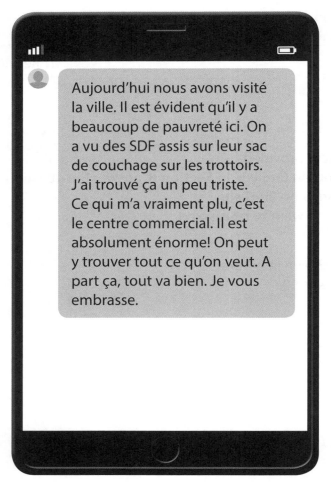

Aujourd'hui nous avons visité la ville. Il est évident qu'il y a beaucoup de pauvreté ici. On a vu des SDF assis sur leur sac de couchage sur les trottoirs. J'ai trouvé ça un peu triste. Ce qui m'a vraiment plu, c'est le centre commercial. Il est absolument énorme! On peut y trouver tout ce qu'on veut. A part ça, tout va bien. Je vous embrasse.

Complete the sentences in **English**.

| 0 | 1 | . | 1 | Arthur saw _____ sitting on the pavement.

[1 mark]

| 0 | 1 | . | 2 | What impressed Arthur in town was _____ .

[1 mark]

| 0 | 2 |

A gap year

You read these contributions to a French online forum on the value of taking a gap year.

Arnaud
Prendre une année sabbatique pour voyager? Moi, je vois ça comme une occasion de me rendre utile. Il y a tant de pauvreté dans le monde. S'il est possible d'aider les gens dans le besoin, à mon avis, il faut le faire. Evidemment, en partant pour un an, on risque de perdre le contact avec ses amis.

Magalie
Il faut reconnaître que c'est une aventure qui coûte les yeux de la tête! Pourtant, c'est à ne pas manquer. En visitant des pays qu'on ne connait pas, on élargit ses horizons et on acquiert une perspective différente du reste du monde.

For each person, write down **one** advantage and **one** disadvantage they mention about taking a gap year.

Complete the boxes in **English**.

| 0 | 2 | . | 1 | Arnaud

Advantage	Disadvantage

[2 marks]

| 0 | 2 | . | 2 | Magalie

Advantage	Disadvantage

[2 marks]

0 3   **The consequences of unemployment**

Read this French article on the consequences of losing one's job.

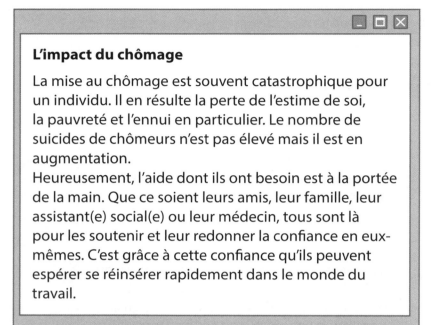

L'impact du chômage

La mise au chômage est souvent catastrophique pour un individu. Il en résulte la perte de l'estime de soi, la pauvreté et l'ennui en particulier. Le nombre de suicides de chômeurs n'est pas élevé mais il est en augmentation.

Heureusement, l'aide dont ils ont besoin est à la portée de la main. Que ce soient leurs amis, leur famille, leur assistant(e) social(e) ou leur médecin, tous sont là pour les soutenir et leur redonner la confiance en eux-mêmes. C'est grâce à cette confiance qu'ils peuvent espérer se réinsérer rapidement dans le monde du travail.

Write the correct letter in each box.

0 3 . 1   According to the article, one of the consequences of losing one's job is …

A	annoyance.
B	a loss of self-esteem.
C	a loss of individuality.

[1 mark]

0 3 . 2   A small but increasing number of unemployed people …

A	are depressed.
B	commit suicide.
C	have dependents to look after.

[1 mark]

▶ **Continued**

0 3 . 3 Through the support given to unemployed people, they will …

A	make new friends.
B	be guaranteed to find a new job.
C	regain their self-confidence.

[1 mark]

0 4   **School improvements**

You read this list of school improvements put together by students.

On devrait …

A avoir des profs de langues qui sont nés dans le pays dont on apprend la langue.

B être libres de choisir toutes les matières qu'on étudie.

C être libres le mercredi après-midi et le weekend.

D faire ses devoirs seulement si on veut.

E pouvoir porter ce qu'on veut d'un point de vue vestimentaire.

F avoir le choix de se présenter aux examens ou non.

G avoir le droit de se plaindre des profs.

H pouvoir fumer dans la cour de récréation.

Which changes would the following people most like to see?

Write the correct letter in the box.

0 4 . 1   We should go down to four and a half days of lessons a week.

[1 mark]

0 4 . 2   I wish I didn't have to take lessons in subjects I'm not interested in.

[1 mark]

0 4 . 3   It would be good to have a Spanish teacher who comes from Spain.

[1 mark]

0 4 . 4   I should be able to tell someone about a teacher who is treating me unfairly.

[1 mark]

0 5   **Staying in good health**

You read this leaflet that advises French people on potential health problems.

A	*Les matières grasses.* Les viandes en contiennent beaucoup. Le problème de l'obésité s'aggrave dans beaucoup de pays du monde.
B	*Les produits qui contiennent un gros pourcentage de sucre.* Que ce soient les biscuits, le chocolat ou les glaces par exemple, le sucre et les matières grasses en sont les principaux composants.
C	*La fatigue.* Le manque de sommeil affecte un grand nombre de personnes. Leur productivité au travail en est amoindrie.
D	*Le tabac sous toutes ses formes.* C'est la raison principale des cancers du poumon.
E	*L'abus des boissons alcoolisées.* Elles affectent nos capacités et nous mettent quelquefois en situations dangereuses.
F	*La drogue.* Elle a un effet sur notre sens de la réalité et il est facile d'en devenir accro.

Read the following advice. Which health problem does each one address?

Write the correct letter in the box.

0 5 . 1   Avoid addictive substances.   ☐

0 5 . 2   Cut down on sugary desserts.   ☐

0 5 . 3   Don't take up smoking.   ☐

0 5 . 4   If possible, avoid butter, oil and red meat, for example.   ☐

0 5 . 5   Have a glass of wine if you like, but only one.   ☐

0 5 . 6   Don't go to bed too late.   ☐

[6 marks]

| 0 | 6 | **Learning foreign languages**

You read this French online article on the importance of learning languages.

Pourquoi apprendre une langue étrangère?

Comment peut-on se débrouiller dans un pays étranger s'il nous est impossible de communiquer? On peut espérer que les gens à qui on parle notre langue comprennent ce qu'on leur dit mais ce n'est pas toujours le cas. Considérons aussi le cas inverse. Si un étranger se trouvant dans notre pays ne parle pas bien notre langue, il est gratifiant de pouvoir l'aider à s'exprimer.

Au niveau professionnel, la connaissance des langues est un atout non négligeable, qui nous permet par exemple de devenir enseignant ou traducteur. Les entreprises qui exportent leurs marchandises ont aussi besoin de quelqu'un capable de négocier leurs transactions.

Cette connaissance est donc un outil utile dans de nombreuses circonstances et il est important quel que soit notre âge d'apprendre les langues étrangères.

Are these statements true (**T**), false (**F**) or not mentioned (**NM**) in the text above?

Write **T**, **F** or **NM** in each box.

| 0 | 6 | . | 1 | While abroad, we cannot assume that people will understand us when we speak our own language.

[1 mark]

| 0 | 6 | . | 2 | It is rewarding to be able to help foreign visitors to our country who do not speak our language well.

[1 mark]

| 0 | 6 | . | 3 | If you want a career using your languages, you have to become either a teacher or a translator.

[1 mark]

| 0 | 6 | . | 4 | In the world of industry, the ability to speak foreign languages is an important asset.

[1 mark]

| 0 | 6 | . | 5 | Everyone is capable of learning a foreign language.

[1 mark]

| 0 | 7 | **Proposal for town improvements**

You read this proposal by a French local council to improve local facilities.

> Nous proposons de construire un centre médical à la sortie de la ville. Celui-ci regrouperait tous les médecins actuellement installés au centre-ville. Nous savons tous qu'il est pratiquement impossible de se garer en ville. Le nouveau centre faciliterait donc l'accès à ceux qui ont de la difficulté à marcher.
> Ce centre comprendrait aussi un cabinet dentaire, un oculiste et une pharmacie. Nous voulons également inclure un petit supermarché et deux ou trois autres petits magasins. Le loyer payé par ces magasins nous aiderait en effet à financer ce projet.

Answer the questions in **English**.

| 0 | 7 | . | 1 | Where is the new medical centre to be built?

_____

[1 mark]

| 0 | 7 | . | 2 | What is the main reason for building it there?

_____

[1 mark]

| 0 | 7 | . | 3 | Why is the construction of small shops included in the project?

_____

[1 mark]

0 8   **A letter from Nice**

Read this extract from the novel '*Un sac de billes*' by Joseph Joffo.

Quatre jours après le retour d'Henri, nous recevions la première lettre en provenance de Nice. Papa se débrouillait bien. Il avait trouvé un appartement dans un quartier un peu écarté près de l'église de la Buffa, il avait loué deux chambres à l'étage au-dessus et il s'était renseigné: il serait facile à Albert et Henri de trouver du travail dans un salon de la ville. Lui aussi travaillerait bien sûr. La saison approchait, il allait y avoir du monde. Dans des lignes assez amères, papa nous apprenait en effet que malgré les "malheurs qui s'étaient abattus sur la France", les palaces, le casino, les boîtes de nuit étaient pleins à craquer et que décidément, la guerre n'existait que pour les pauvres. Il terminait en nous demandant de patienter encore et il pensait que d'ici un ou deux mois, il nous serait possible de venir. Nous serions alors à nouveau réunis comme autrefois, comme à Paris.

Answer the questions in **English**.

0 8 . 1   Which member of the family is already in Nice?

_____

[1 mark]

0 8 . 2   What accommodation was he able to secure? Give **two** details.

_____

[2 marks]

0 8 . 3   What else will be easy to find in Nice?

_____

[1 mark]

▶ **Continued**

08 . 4   What makes the father think that the poor are more affected by the war than the rich?

_____

[1 mark]

08 . 5   When does the father expect the whole family to be back together again?

_____

[1 mark]

Section B   Questions and answers in **French**

| 0 | 9 |

Le portable: ses bienfaits et ses dangers

Lisez ces commentaires en ligne sur les bienfaits et les dangers du téléphone portable.

A	Si je risque d'oublier un rendez-vous, mon téléphone me le rappelle. **Henri**	**E**	On peut avoir la réponse à n'importe quelle question. **Gabriel**
B	Ça rend la vie plus facile. Il n'y a aucun doute là-dessus. **Marie**	**F**	Si on y passe trop de temps, il est possible qu'on ne réussira pas à ses examens. **Magalie**
C	On peut se laisser séduire. **Julie**	**G**	Ça permet de ne pas perdre le contact avec ceux qu'on connait. **Roger**
D	Il est certain que ça abime les yeux. **Eric**	**H**	Ça peut avoir un mauvais effet sur la santé. **Hélène**

Identifiez les **quatre** dangers. Ecrivez les bonnes lettres dans les cases.

☐   ☐   ☐   ☐

[4 marks]

| 1 | 0 | La séparation des couples

Lisez cet article tiré d'un magazine français sur les effets de la séparation des couples.

> En France, selon les statistiques, un mariage sur deux finit en divorce. C'est sans aucun doute un chiffre à la fois impressionnant et inquiétant. Chez les couples qui vivent en concubinage, le taux de séparation est le même que chez les couples mariés. Il semblerait alors que le mariage n'apporte pas aux jeunes mariés la sécurité qu'ils en attendent.
>
> Pour les couples sans enfants, c'est une décision qui ne concerne qu'eux-mêmes. Les enfants de parents séparés, toutefois, font alors soit partie d'une famille monoparentale soit acquièrent un beau-père ou une belle-mère et peut-être aussi des demi-frères ou des demi-sœurs. S'ils arrivent tous à s'entendre, ça va, mais ce n'est malheureusement pas toujours le cas.
>
> De plus, le parent qui n'est plus là leur manque et c'est une réaction tout à fait normale. Lorsqu'un couple se sépare, il n'est pas toujours conscient des conséquences de cette décision.

Complétez les phrases en **français**.

| 1 | 0 | . | 1 | En France, dans _____ pour cent des cas, les couples finissent par se séparer.

[1 mark]

| 1 | 0 | . | 2 | Les couples qui ne sont pas mariés vivent _____.

[1 mark]

| 1 | 0 | . | 3 | La decision de divorcer a moins de conséquences pour les couples sans

_____.

[1 mark]

| 1 | 0 | . | 4 | Les enfants de notre beau-père ou belle-mère sont nos

_____.

[1 mark]

| 1 | 0 | . | 5 | Ce qui manque le plus aux enfants dont les parents sont séparés,

c'est leur _____.

[1 mark]

| 1 | 1 | | **Les changements climatiques** |

Lisez cet extrait d'un magazine scientifique français sur les effets du changement climatique.

Nous savons tous que les émissions de dioxyde de carbone contribuent à l'effet de serre qui est la cause du réchauffement de la terre. Pourquoi devrait-on s'en inquiéter? Parce que cela implique la fonte des glaciers, en particulier dans les régions polaires, et donc la montée du niveau des mers et des océans. De nos jours, certaines îles risquent d'être submergées. Dans d'autres régions du monde, cette hausse des températures est associée à la sécheresse et aux feux de forêts.

Que peut-on y faire? Il est absolument nécessaire que chaque pays apporte une solution à ces problèmes. Les gouvernements et les industries ont leur rôle à jouer. Les individus aussi! A la maison, chacun doit essayer de réduire sa consommation d'énergie en économisant le gaz, l'électricité et l'eau. A part cela, il est fortement recommandé d'utiliser les transports en commun tels que le train, le bus ou le tramway plutôt que sa voiture et aussi d'éviter de voyager en avion.

Choisissez les **quatre** phrases qui sont vraies. Ecrivez les bonnes lettres dans les cases.

A	Le réchauffement de la terre est la cause de l'effet de serre.
B	Si les temperatures montent, les glaciers fondent.
C	Dans les régions polaires, le niveau des mers monte moins rapidement.
D	Les petites îles en particulier sont en danger.
E	La sécheresse et les feux de forêts sont de graves problèmes en France.
F	Les changements climatiques concernent tous les pays du monde.
G	Chez soi, chacun doit faire un effort afin de consommer moins d'énergie.
H	Il vaut mieux voyager en avion plutôt qu'en train.

[ ] [ ] [ ] [ ]

[4 marks]

1 2   **Comment éviter le stress des examens**

Lisez ces conseils de révisions à des élèves français.

A	Ne passez pas toute la journée à réviser. Arrêtez-vous de temps en temps et reposez-vous.

B	Ne vous couchez pas trop tard.

C	Préparez un emploi du temps pour vos révisions et adhérez-y.

D	Assurez-vous d'avoir huit heures de sommeil par jour.

E	Révisez un maximum de deux matières chaque jour.

A quel conseil ces phrases correspondent-elles?

Ecrivez la bonne lettre dans chaque case.

1 2 . 1   Je dois suivre mon programme de révision de près.

[1 mark]

1 2 . 2   Je ferai des pauses régulièrement, probablement toutes les deux heures.

[1 mark]

1 2 . 3   Je vais aller au lit de bonne heure.

[1 mark]

1 2 . 4   Il ne faut pas que j'étudie trop de matières à la fois.

[1 mark]

1 2 . 5   Il faut que je m'endorme vers vingt-trois heures et que je me lève vers sept heures.

[1 mark]

Section C   Translation into **English**

1 3   Your friend has seen this post on social media and asks you to translate it for him into English.

> «Restez célibataires. C'est la seule manière de pouvoir faire ce que vous voulez.» C'est ce que nous conseillent la plupart de ceux qui se sont séparés de leur partenaire. Il se pourrait que ce soit vrai mais quand on aime quelqu'un, ce qui compte le plus, c'est de vivre heureux ensemble.

[9 marks]

_____

_____

_____

_____

_____

_____

_____

_____

END OF QUESTIONS

Answers and mark schemes

Higher Tier Paper 4 Writing

Time allowed: 1 hour 15 minutes

Instructions

- You must answer **three** questions.
- You must answer **either** Question 1.1 **or** Question 1.2. Do not answer both of these questions.
- You must answer **either** Question 2.1 **or** Question 2.2. Do not answer both of these questions.
- You must answer Question 3.
- Answer all questions in **French**.
- Answer the questions in the spaces provided.
- Cross through any work you do not want to be marked.

Information

- The marks for the questions are shown in brackets.
- The maximum mark for this paper is 60.
- You must **not** use a dictionary during this test.
- In order to score the highest marks for Question 1.1/Question 1.2, you must write something about each bullet point. You must use a variety of vocabulary and structures and include your opinions.
- In order to score the highest marks for Question 2.1/Question 2.2, you must write something about both bullet points. You must use a variety of vocabulary and structures and include your opinions and reasons.

Please note: The Practice Paper questions and answers have not been written or approved by AQA.

Answer **either** Question 1.1 **or** Question 1.2.
You must **not** answer **both** of these questions.

EITHER Question 1.1

| 0 | 1 |.| 1 | Vous décrivez votre régime alimentaire à votre ami(e) français(e).

Décrivez:

- ce que vous prenez pour le petit déjeuner
- votre attitude en ce qui concerne les régimes végétarien et végétalien
- votre dernier repas au restaurant
- ce que vous ferez à l'avenir pour éviter l'obésité.

Ecrivez environ **90** mots en **français**. Répondez à chaque aspect de la question.   **[16 marks]**

OR Question 1.2

| 0 | 1 |.| 2 | Vous décrivez votre région à votre ami(e) français(e).

Décrivez:

- votre ville
- ce que vous avez fait le weekend dernier en ville
- ce qu'il y a de beau dans votre région
- ce que vous ferez dans votre région pendant les vacances scolaires.

Ecrivez environ **90** mots en **français**. Répondez à chaque aspect de la question.   **[16 marks]**

Answer **either** Question 2.1 **or** Question 2.2.
You must **not** answer **both** of these questions.

EITHER Question 2.1

| 0 | 2 | . | 1 | Vous décrivez vos soucis environnementaux à votre ami(e) français(e).

Décrivez:

- les problèmes de l'environnement qui vous inquiètent

- les solutions possibles à ces problèmes.

Ecrivez environ **150** mots en **français**. Répondez aux deux aspects de la question.   **[32 marks]**

OR Question 2.2

| 0 | 2 | . | 2 | Vous décrivez vos hésitations en ce qui concerne votre avenir professionnel à votre ami(e) français(e).

Décrivez:

- votre indécision en ce qui concerne votre avenir professionnel

- les conseils donnés par le conseiller d'éducation.

Ecrivez environ **150** mots en **français**. Répondez aux deux aspects de la question.   **[32 marks]**

0	3

Translate the following passage into **French**.

> I have always liked sport. When I was younger, I used to play football with all my friends. Now, I am part of the school team. We train twice a week. Next Saturday, we will play against another school. In my opinion, it is the best of all team sports.

[12 marks]

_____

_____

_____

_____

_____

_____

_____

_____

_____

_____

_____

_____

_____

END OF QUESTIONS

Model answers and mark schemes

AQA GCSE French Higher Practice Papers © Oxford University Press 2020. Photocopying prohibited.

Great Clarendon Street, Oxford, OX2 6DP, United Kingdom

Oxford University Press is a department of the University of Oxford.

It furthers the University's objective of excellence in research, scholarship, and education by publishing worldwide. Oxford is a registered trade mark of Oxford University Press in the UK and in certain other countries

British Library Cataloguing in Publication Data
Data available

978 1 38200694 1

10 9 8 7 6 5 4 3 2 1

Paper used in the production of this book is a natural, recyclable product made from wood grown in sustainable forests. The manufacturing process conforms to the environmental regulations of the country of origin.

Printed in Great Britain by Ashford Colour Press Ltd, Gosport.

Acknowledgements
The publisher and authors would like to thank the following for permission to use photographs:

p23: SolStock/iStockPhoto; **p24:** PeopleImages/iStockPhoto; **p25:** DGLimages/iStockPhoto; **p71:** Monkey Business Images/Shutterstock; **p72:** Tommy Trenchard/Alamy Stock Photo; **p73:** Tetra Images/Getty Images; **p119:** Jacek Chabraszewski/Shutterstock; **p120:** bensliman hassan/Shutterstock; **p121:** monkeybusinessimages/iStockPhoto.

The publisher and author are grateful to the following for permission to reprint extracts from copyright material:

p43: *Bonjour Tristesse*, Françoise Sagan © Éditions Juillard, Paris, 1954, 2014; **p44**: Jacques Prévert, 'Déjeuner du matin', in *Paroles* © Éditions Gallimard; **p88** and **p138**: *Un sac de billes*, Joseph Joffo © Éditions JC Lattès

Although we have made every effort to trace and contact all copyright holders before publication this has not been possible in all cases. If notified, the publisher will rectify any errors or omissions at the earliest opportunity.

Links to third party websites are provided by Oxford in good faith and for information only. Oxford disclaims any responsibility for the materials contained in any third party website referenced in this work.